Succeeding with Difficult Bosses

Joseph E Koob II

Revised Second Edition

ISBN: 9781088694206

A difficultpeople.org publication

Table of Contents

PREFACE

"What personally threatens us is a fear that we will be deprived of what we want the most, to be liked and approved of, to have our achievements recognized, or to be seen by those we respect as competent and in charge." (Bramson)

So much of our appreciation and success at work seems to have to do with who our boss is – as a manager (good or bad), as a leader (one who inspires or does not), and, most importantly, as a person (does he/she care). What we do care the most about in a person who is above us in the chain of command is their willingness (or not) to acknowledge, appreciate, and recognize who we are and the effort we put forth. When people get together and talk about 'difficult' bosses, the root of their concerns is often that they FEEL left out, unappreciated, put down, 'less than,' and treated almost as a non-entity.

This book is focused on understanding the unique relationship we have with a person who has hierarchical power over us. To truly gain the knowledge we need to be successful with difficult bosses, we need to understand who they are as a person and what they do that frustrates us, i.e. the behavior patterns they have that cause us turmoil and upset. We must also understand ourselves – how we subconsciously add to the mix, and how we can change our outlook and behavior so that our boss will change his or her behavior in relationship to us. While there are numerous books available on dealing/working with difficult people, my approach is to present the most comprehensive perspective possible by creating a work that brings together ideas from the 'dealing with difficult people/difficult situations' literature. At the same time, I try to provide a format that is easy to read, practical, and down-to-earth. The primary focus is always on what you can learn and the skills and tools you can practice to be successful with difficult behaviors.

As an author of many books on "Understanding and Working with Difficult People," I try to continue to expand my own understanding with each book I write. The research for this book provided some very interesting and worthwhile sources. See the extensive Bibliography at the end of this work, as well as an Annotated Bibliography of books available at our website: www.difficultpeople.org.

Succeeding with Difficult Bosses represents one book in my Business Trilogy aimed at "Succeeding in the Work Place." The other two books in this series, *Succeeding with Difficult Coworkers* and *Managing with Difficult Employees* Second Editions will be released soon as well.

Please note that the understanding and skills that can be gleaned from this work build from section to section. Many ideas presented in earlier parts of the book are critical to being successful with understanding and dealing with difficult behaviors discussed later in the work. We encourage you to read the entire book and then return to those sections that are of personal relevance to your concerns.

Consider our books, *Understanding and Working with Difficult People*, and *Me! A Difficult Person?* for a comprehensive general approach to difficult people. Both these works provide a foundation upon which to build your skills in working with difficult people.

Addendum

Working with difficult people is often physically taxing and emotionally draining. It is advisable to make sure you are in good physical and emotional health as you set out on your path to success. See Chapter 11, "Taking Care of Yourself," for specific recommendations. It is always advisable to seek professional assistance if you feel your concerns are affecting your personal well-being.

A Word about Gender

Men and women bosses can be equally difficult. I vary the usage of 'him,' 'her,' 'them,' etc. throughout the text. From my experience as a coach, counselor, mentor, and human being, everyone is different, and we can all be difficult at times and in many different ways.

Thanks

Many thanks to all who have continued to encourage us in our endeavors to bring such a wide range of materials to the general public. Especially a hat tip to Heath Potter whose hard work made difficultpeople.org a reality. Brenda Whiteway for her input; my wife and children; and my inveterate, if not brave, readers: Anne Duston, Lisa, Brenda, Steve, and Nathan, who put up with my many little quirks and strange meanderings.

Chapter 1

KEY IDEAS

"It is the attempt, the process, the struggle that counts. Not that I

know why it does – I only know that it does."

(Theodora J. Koob – In Memoriam)

YOU are the Key to Success

Yes, you may have a jerk for a boss – idiot, a control-freak, a manipulator, criticizer, etc. But you can't change them...not directly. You probably wish that you could wave a magic wand and this curmudgeon you work with would suddenly change personalities, or decide to take another job. Unfortunately, these things very rarely happen when we want them to.

Your only means to be successful with this difficult person in your life is to change yourself – and your approach to them.

At difficultpeople.org one of our most oft quoted statements, and a key idea is,

You can only change yourself; you cannot change other people...directly.

If you have a difficult person in your life and you are frustrated because no matter what you seem to do doesn't effect change, **then you need to change what you are doing**. It does take a good bit of effort and time on your part:

Developing an understanding of how to work with difficult authority figures

Understanding your boss and his/her behaviors

Understanding yourself better

Learning skills and tools that will help you make changes that can make a difference

Creating the work-life that works for you

The good news is that in most cases when you use the positive, assertive approach we recommend, you will effect positive change in your relationships with others, at work, and even with an 'Idiot' boss (Hoover, *How to Work for an Idiot*).

Always keep in mind the POWER thing

The approach and tenor of this book is different from all the other books in the difficultpeople.org literature because it focuses exclusively on difficult relationships where one person has some type of influence or power 'over' another.

Bosses are, well, bosses, i.e. "A person in authority over employees..." (Webster). For better, and unfortunately, often for the worse, if you are an employee of a difficult boss, they can affect your evaluations, your success, your enjoyment at work, your effectiveness and quality, your self-worth...your whole life.

It is very important to keep this key idea in mind as you read this book and whenever you are considering how you will approach an authority figure in your life. Our recommendations for success in this book are based on understanding how 'authority' makes a difference.

People use power and control differently, so understanding your boss and how they 'do things' is critical to being successful with them.

Power and control are not always clear-cut in today's business world either. But be assured that in any organization there are levels, and levels create separation – with those layers comes influence. That influence does affect your success as an employee, and it affects your ability to enjoy your work environment as well. Never forget the 'POWER' thing – it may be subtle, but it is there and people do use it as a means of manipulating people and circumstances.

'Difficulty' is in the eyes of the beholder

At difficultpeople.org we define a difficult person as "**anyone who causes anyone else angst.**" This is purposely a very broad definition. It suggests a number of things:

That we are all difficult at times

That what we see as difficult may or may not be seen as difficult to someone else

That our perceptions and the perceptions of others are very important to understanding each other

That people are different – it is the most common cause of angst/difficulties between people

And taking this slightly further, it suggests another Key Idea:

Most people don't know they are difficult.

And, another key point:

If you see someone as difficult, it is VERY likely they will see you as difficult.

Most people don't know they are being difficult

This statement may seem very hard to accept at a gut level. However, even really difficult people often don't have a conception of how they are seen by, or come across, to others. They don't understand themselves.

Self-knowledge is a very powerful tool (**Self-Awareness**, is one of the *Seven Keys to Being Successful with Difficult People*, see next page). When you understand yourself, you bring much more self-control into a difficult situation with another person. It can make a major difference in how you approach them.

Difficult People often (very often) see other people as being difficult

The very nature of the poor self-image of a very difficult person lends itself to projecting blame and negativity onto many of the people they interact with. When someone doesn't feel positive about who they are and how they appear, they tend to project those feelings onto others – so the people that they employ feel unappreciated, undervalued, talked down to, argued with, etc.

It is important to keep this key idea in mind as you work with your 'difficult' boss. He/she does not perceive the world, you, or himself, as you do. These differences in perspective dramatically affect your interactions with him. When one person makes an effort to understand another, this mis-balance of perspectives changes, and the dynamics of the relationship will also likely begin to change. You can be the catalyst for positive change by understanding that these dynamics exist between you and your boss and by making an effort to understand your boss (See Chapter 9, "Knowing Your Boss")

The Seven Keys

(to being Successful with Difficult People)

Over the course of developing many books and articles about difficult people, I have developed a list of seven **Key Ideas** that are relevant to all difficult people concerns. The next seven chapters will be devoted to discussing these at length.

Take a few moments to consider how these ideas may be key to your relationship with your boss:

Self-Awareness

Self-worth

Self-Confidence

Self-Control

Honesty

Kindness

Positivity

Knowledge IS a powerful tool

Self-awareness, the first of the "Keys to being Successful with Difficult People," focuses first on "Knowing Yourself," and how everything you do, say, think, feel, etc. impacts your life with another person. While you may feel you have a good fundamental perspective of who you are and how you come across to others, the truth is we can all learn a great deal more about how we impact the world and people around us. Self-awareness is an ongoing commitment to knowing ourselves and to being the person we want to be.

The other side of the coin is making an effort to understand the other person. The more you can understand what is driving your boss' behavior, the better you will be able to handle the situation in a positive and constructive manner for all concerned.

There are many personal dynamics that are created when two people interact on a regular basis. You can make a difference in your relationship with the authority figures in your life by understand yourself and by making an effort to understand who they are and how they approach their work and life. This book encourages you to set a lifelong goal of understanding yourself better so that your interactions with others help you to be the positive, in-control person you want to bring to the fore.

Dealing with Behaviors

This book focuses on being successful with difficult behaviors exhibited by authority figures in your life. We are all people; we all have the right to be successful and content at work. When we have to endure difficult behaviors from another person, particularly an authority figure, we tend to react in ways that are primarily defensive and protective. By understanding the specific behaviors that cause us angst we can separate the person from their 'difficultness.' We can work with and be successful with behaviors – it is much harder to successful with an 'idiot' or an...fill-in-the-blank.

> Note: How you perceive your difficult boss can be very telling in and of itself. Rather than using a generic, all-encompassing term to describe them, try delineating the things that frustrate you about how they approach you.

> This is an excellent exercise – consider taking some time to write out specific behaviors, attributes, ways your boss treats and approaches you. You will gain insight into your boss and how he/she pushes your buttons.

Being able to focus, very specifically, on what really is troubling you about someone, their negative behaviors, opens the doors for learning to be successful with them.

You have the POWER

We truly believe that you can make a major difference in your relationship with a difficult authority figure. We always advocate a positive, knowledge-based, self-controlled approach to working with difficult others. You can choose other approaches, but you will feel better about your life and work if you make a personal commitment to self-improvement and positivity.

Yes, there are some REALLY difficult bosses out there (see Chapters 23 and 24). Even they can be affected in a positive way by the ideas, techniques, and skills recommended in this book. Keep in mind, however, that your safety and well-being and that of others is of paramount concern. If you feel the situation is beyond your control and/or dangerous, please get help.

Questions and Ideas for Contemplation

As you go through the rest of this book you will see the ideas presented in this chapter in many different forms. Take some time to review all the key ideas above while considering your relationship with your boss. It can be very helpful to jot down some of your thoughts as you do this exercise. Refer back to your notes as you read the rest of this book. You will find that your insight will expand as you go.

Suggestion: Go back over each of these key statements (section titles and bold print) several times and consider what they mean to you and your relationship with your 'difficult' boss. They can have a fundamental impact on our understanding and in our ability to adjust our own behavior in order to be successful with difficult others. For further discussion centered on these ideas see, *Understanding and Working with Difficult People*, and *Succeeding with Difficult Coworkers*. (Koob.)

Go to www.difficultpeople.org for more information and resources about *Understanding and Working with Difficult People*. We encourage you to peruse as much as possible. There is an extensive bibliography at the end of this book listing many informative additional readings, including a bibliography of Dr. Koob's "difficult people" books.

Chapter 2

SELF-AWARENESS

"Know Thyself." (Socrates)

"To be aware of a single shortcoming within oneself is more

useful than to be aware of a thousand in somebody else."

(The Dalai Lama)

Self-awareness is the first of the "Seven Keys to being Successful with Difficult People."

Your Foundation for Success

YOU are the key to being successful with difficult people. The better you understand yourself the better you will be able to control how interactions go with everyone you deal with on a day-to-day basis. Your self-knowledge and the confidence that comes with truly understanding yourself is especially useful in working with those who are in a position of authority over you.

To fully understand yourself you should:

Know your strengths (and use them to your advantage)

Know your weaknesses (so you can work on them and make allowances/changes when you need to)

Know how other people's approach to you, i.e. their actions, words, body language, etc., affect you

Know how you feel, think, react, act in difficult situations

Know how your reactions and actions affect other people

Know how other people perceive you

Have a good sense of who you truly are as a person, both outwardly in the day-to-day world, and inwardly – the person you truly want to be

Know your strengths

We all have things we are good at. You may not feel that way when you are dealing directly with a very negative, critical authority figure, but deep inside, you know. It is important that every day we acknowledge ourselves for the many good points we have, despite any negativity around us.

"Nobody's good at everything, but everybody's good at something." (Concerned Children's Advertising)

Negative people tend to focus predominantly on the mistakes we make and the lapses we may occasionally have in our work:

I once had a very critical, nit-picking boss. If I made one mistake in a hundred-page report, I would hear about only that. I never heard anything about the excellent job I did in bringing all the materials together and writing this monstrosity of a document, just the few negative things he could find. **However**, I knew I was a good writer and that I had done an excellent job. (Which was later proved by the success of the project, as a direct result of the document I produced.)

Does this scenario sound familiar? It goes back to our need for appreciation, acknowledgement, and recognition, as well basic human kindness and compassion.

Acknowledge yourself for your strengths, and use them to your advantage. If you are good at writing and bringing diverse ideas together into a whole, volunteer for that kind of work. Shine the way you know you can shine. There are almost always opportunities every day to use our strengths to advantage.

Know your weaknesses

We also all have things that we would like to be able to do better or with more ease. Rather than put yourself down for those things you could be better at, stay on top of your 'inadequacies' and make allowances by being extra vigilant, extra careful, and by seeking help and support when needed.

Just as I feel I am a good writer, capable of organizing huge amounts of data and ideas into a cohesive whole, I also know I am not the best detail person. I deal with this 'weakness' in several ways:

> I get help with this area by using readers for almost everything I write – people who are detail people.

> I read, re-read, re-re-read, and re-re-re-read, etc., everything I write. I still don't catch everything, but it helps me be better than I would normally be at detail work.

> I use every source I can to help me overcome this problem (spell checker, grammar checker, dictionary, thesaurus), especially my own self-worth and patience. I accept the weakness, but I also deal with it as successfully as I can.

Pay Attention!

These two words may be the most important phrase associated with being successful with difficult people. To understand ourselves fully we must be willing to look, very carefully and very honestly, at who we are, how we interact with others, and how others are affected by our actions and words.

Do you really know yourself?

"There are three Things extreamly (sic) hard, Steel, a Diamond, and to know one's self."
(Benjamin Franklin)

The truth is, most of us don't know ourselves or how we come across to others very well. We can only know who we are and how we impact others if we are willing to observe our feelings, thoughts, actions, reactions, etc. It takes considerable practice and a good bit of bravery to do this on a daily basis.

Most people don't know how they impact others. It is a basic understanding we need to have in working with difficult people – most people who are regularly and even pervasively negative to others, have no clue as to how they come across. They see themselves in an entirely different light.

How to know yourself?

Especially when faced with difficulties?

Start with basic self-observation in everyday situations. Ask yourself:

How am I feeling?

What am I thinking?

How am I impelled to react to what this person is saying/doing?

What about their behavior is 'setting me off.'

How do I typically react?

What actions do I take?

How do I feel afterward and what impact have my reactions/actions had on me and others?

What could I have done differently for this situation to have a more positive outcome for me?

When you can stop yourself from automatically reacting in a negative situation, and self-observe, you have taken a major step forward in being able to handle that (and other) difficult concerns. Then you will have the power to make more positive choices for yourself. You will need to commit to practicing self-observation techniques for an extended period of time, so it becomes an automatic response in difficult situations with others.

How do other people see YOU?

If you see someone as being difficult, it is VERY likely that they see YOU as being difficult. Perceptions are everything. We may be a very nice, calm, easy-going person, but if the other person sees us in a different light, **then that's who we are to them** and no amount of arguing with them will change their mind.

Knowing, through careful observation how your interactions with others go, and how someone perceives you, i.e. your communications, reactions, responses, etc, is critical to your being successful in difficult encounters. This takes not only paying attention to yourself, but also paying close attention to the other person and how they respond to you. This is an important way to begin to understand what the other person is bringing to the equation of your interpersonal relations with them. The more you understand your difficult boss, the better you will be able to deal successfully with him. (See also Chapter 9, "Knowing Your Boss")

It goes back to those two key words, **"Paying Attention**." As you observe yourself and others you gain self-understanding and you gain self-control. Pay attention to yourself and others; you will experience tremendous personal growth as a result.

Your true self

I truly believe that we all have the right to be the best we can be, and part of that process is accepting that our life's responsibilities rests firmly on our own shoulders. Through whatever difficulties arise, we have to make the best choices for who we are and who we want to become.

Ask yourself

Who am I and how do I fit into the grand scheme of things?

You can approach this from several perspectives:

Who am I? Deep inside? The real me?

Who do I really want to be?

How am I bringing this conception to reality in this world (at home, at work, with friends)?

Can I bring the inner reality/dream of who I truly want to be to outward fruition?

I believe the best way to get at who you are fundamentally as a human being, the 'true' you, is to do a little exercise I developed for my book *Guiding Children*.

Who we are fundamentally is based on what we really value. If we consider the qualities that we would want our children to have and develop as they grow up, I believe we are touching on what we truly value in ourselves. Try this exercise:

What ten qualities or values would you like to instill in your children as they grow?

Make a list.

Try to be specific and to keep the number at or below ten fundamental qualities. Stick with values and qualities, i.e. don't put in things like, "I want John to be an eminent surgeon."

When you have a solid list, start to prioritize. Pick the top five values you would like them to have; then narrow it to three. See if you can get it down to the one most important, fundamental quality you would like your child to have. Then put the list back together in order of priority.

Chances are this list describes what your ideal of YOU is.

Need help getting started? Make a list of values and qualities you admire in general. Things like: Honesty, Caring, Trustworthy, Conscientious, Generous, Humble, and so on. Write down as many as you think of and then take a break. Keep adding to your list for a period of time (week?). When you feel you have a comprehensive list, narrow it down to those you value the most for your children, AND for yourself.

Find the best words that work for your personal vision of the best YOU.

After you have developed your list, print it out and carry it with you or post it in a place where you will encounter it frequently. You can also make a small-print version, laminate it, and carry it in your wallet or purse.

Another Perspective

Another means of understanding what you truly value is to ask your self-these questions:

How would you like your life to be remembered?

What would you like engraved on your tombstone – the final comment on who you were?

These are very personal considerations and you may find thinking about them a bit difficult, but when we are willing to make the effort, it does help us focus on what is most important. If you feel it could help, you could discuss this approach with a close friend or relative. When we consider these types of questions, it places our whole life in perspective, and can give us a fundamental ideal or concept to continually strive for.

Here's the clincher

In every interaction you have,

How are you manifesting the qualities of your ideal you?

How do you bring what you value most to the fore?

How many moments of your existence from this point on can you live fulfilling this personal image?

The more you can be you, the you of your deepest values and qualities, the easier your relationships with difficult others will be...and the more joyous and fulfilling your life will be, too.

Questions and Ideas for Contemplation

Take time today to closely observe your interaction with another person (any person, they don't have to be difficult). What do you see about yourself, what do you notice about the other person? You may feel that this will interfere with your spontaneity, but the truth is we all can do this very effectively without much effort.

Take this a step further by observing yourself in a difficult/emotional interaction. You will find that as you step back and observe your feelings, thoughts, involvement, potential reactions and actual reactions, that you have made an important shift toward better self-control. That little pause of self-observation gives you the opportunity, if you choose, to make different, more positive choices for yourself. Much of the second part of this book will focus on the better choices you can make.

Choose to begin your new life as a courageous, in-control employee by becoming more self-aware and hence more self-reliant.

Chapter 3

SELF-WORTH

"Your success when working with difficult peers and difficult people in positions of power all comes down to attitude – yours." (Hoover)

Who are you at work?

Are you...

> Unhappy, Depressed
>
> Frustrated
>
> Emotionally drained
>
> Angry
>
> Rejected, Hurt
>
> Resentful
>
> Humiliated
>
> Tense, Stressed, Anxious

Do you...

> Complain a lot?
>
> Worry and Whine?
>
> Blame others, 'them,' your boss, 'the company,' for troubles at work
>
> Find yourself being defensive a lot

Or are you…

> Happy

> Positive, Light-hearted

> Easy-going

> Solution-oriented, Proactive

> Supportive

> Responsible

Negativity means your self-worth has taken a hit

> Egotism is trying to prove we are significant/important; self-worth is knowing we are significant and being content with that.

> "Everyone has feelings of inferiority to some degree." (Meier)

Self-worth is about how we feel about ourselves on a minute-by-minute basis. It is different from egotism, which has more to do with weighing our value against others and is heavily invested in how others perceive us. Self-worth is about how we value ourselves and in extension how we value others. If we value who we are at the core of our being, and bring that to the fore, especially when dealing with difficult situations, we begin to bring those values and qualities into our daily life and in our interactions with others.

Our ego plays another game entirely. It helps us accept the negativity of others; it encourages us to fight back and defend ourselves; and it makes sure we dredge up old feelings of rejection, poor self-worth, lack of confidence and self-control, and other many unconstructive/destructive emotions in our dealings with others.

Ego plays a huge role in our business lives, and you can be assured it is playing a major role in your life with a difficult boss. Learn to trust yourself and what you value and avoid the negativity your ego dredges up to devalue you with respect to others.

Self-awareness supports our Self-worth

When we practice self-awareness, we can learn to recognize almost instantly when our thoughts and emotions become less than positive. By paying attention to ourselves throughout the day, we can bring any negativity that begins to creep in up short by simply recognizing when it starts to impact us. Over time we can strengthen our belief in our self and our own values and qualities by avoiding negativity and choosing positivity instead. (see Chapter 8)

It takes time and effort

Changing negative patterns of behavior, i.e., poor or inadequate feelings about ourselves, doesn't happen overnight. Most of us have long-ingrained, deeply imbedded feelings of inadequacy. We were taught, throughout our lives, by people we cared about and people we encountered that we weren't 'good enough,' that we were 'less than,' because we didn't measure up to 'X' or 'Y'. It is the very rare person indeed who has grown up in a completely positive and supportive environment.

Changing old feelings and deep-rooted pain by **paying attention** does work. You can help your self-growth along by not only catching your negative self-talk and feelings, but by reversing self-talk through positive affirmations. If you are feeling 'less than,' negative, and/or inadequate, because of some encounter or experience, make yourself shift gears:

> "Mary, you idiot, you can never get anything right." [Boss fuming at you because you made a small error on a chart.]

> Typical self-talk: "I can't believe I missed that. What a loser I am. Why couldn't I have seen that? Now I'm in the dog house again. I never get it right. I don't know what is wrong with me...." [And so on... you probably know your own drill quite well.]

> Much better: "Lyle, I did miss that. I'm sorry. I will fix it immediately. I'm glad you caught it. However, I think you will find that the report is very well done and it should give us a strong position with Greg (Lyle's boss) when we get to the budget hearings." Then, she adds to herself, "I know this is really well done. I made a huge effort and you can see it in the quality. I can't believe I missed that one item though. I will have to ask Andy to double-check my work next time before I send it up to Lyle. Lyle will see what a great job I did when we get the money we requested for this project...."

If you take a close look at these examples, you will see quite a few important dynamics centered around a difficult situation and positive self-worth. **First and foremost is getting away from typical self-put-down behavior.** Even if you made a mistake, you have value, and you know it. Secondly, in spite of her boss' negative behavior, Mary admits her mistake, accepts responsibility, is proactive about making it good, and is assertive in stating that she feels she did a good job. She accepts herself and acknowledges herself for her own work.

Yes, she may still have some negative feelings about making the mistake and not catching it, but she is positive about dealing with it. This is far better than wallowing in negativity because one's ego has taken a hit. Over time her self-worth will build, and these types of difficult situations will have less and less negative impact on her day and life. It is also quite likely that Mary's boss will notice that she has taken a different tack and that he will respect her more because she is willing to stand up for her own quality.

Take charge of the things you say to yourself (Brinkman and Kirschner)

When you are able to monitor your own self-talk and feelings, you do have the ability to reverse the negative self-programming you have developed and used for many years. If you don't, you will continue to undermine your sense of self-worth. (Meier) It does take some effort to get in the habit of catching your self-deprecating talk, but once you reach the stage where you can STOP negative self-talk as soon as you begin to disparage yourself, you can begin to find more positive and supportive ways to say things to yourself. This type of practice infects others as well, because any negativity we have within will eventually leak out in some form or another.

"When you change the way you talk to yourself about a problem, you change the way you think about it at the same time." (Brinkman and Kirschner)

Difficulties, anxieties, concerns, and negativity in general can dissipate rapidly when you make a daily effort to change, through careful self-observation, less-than-positive thought patterns. A key factor is to recognize when you are not feeling positive and to ask yourself, 'Why do I feel bad?' 'What's going on here?' Then you can see how you are deprecating yourself, or others, or blaming and complaining about work, your organization, 'them,' life, etc.

Remember, "Negativity breeds Negativity." When you are feeling bad about yourself, that can infect everything you do and everyone you interact with at work and outside of work. Reversing negative self-talk can make a major difference over time in how you feel and how you are perceived by others.

Stop being a victim

Far too often we are victims of our own negative thinking.

Take charge of YOU!

Make a decision to begin to shift to a more positive, proactive means of dealing with life. You can only be responsible for yourself. When you accept that responsibility, regardless of what problems and negativity come your way, the whole world can change for you. When we don't accept responsibility, we end up wallowing in pain, anxiety, blame, etc. In other words, we are a **victim** of circumstances or a **victim** of our boss, or a **victim** of 'them.'

Take responsibility for YOUR life.

Hint: you can't do that when you are blaming others.

Here is an interesting question:

What is the opposite of a victim?

Can you envision what being a 'non-victim' would be like?

A valuable alternate perspective

When we put ourselves down, we are very likely doing the same thing to others. (Markham; Koob) Even if it is only inside our heads, what we think and feel leaks out in many ways: through our attitude to others, our approach, our body language, the intonation of our voice, avoidance, etc.

Changing our own inner thoughts and feelings impacts everyone in many ways. It goes back to our fundamental roots: Who do we really want to be? How do others perceive us?

When your self-worth does take a hit

It seems almost inevitable, especially if we have to deal regularly with a negative person, that we will face some adjustments and even major hits to our self-worth (and our ego then jumps on the bandwagon to protect us). Having to deal with change, extreme negativity from others, and difficulties in life in general all can affect how we feel about ourselves. When this happens, do yourself a favor and take a step back and appreciate yourself for who you are and all of your strengths and positive qualities. (also see Chapter 11, "Taking Care of You")

It is also valuable to go back to your fundamental roots from time to time to revisit the basic values and qualities that you believe in (see Chapter 2 for this exercise).

> Every time I do this I smile inside. Because then I am able to focus on who I really am. And though sometimes I get off base or a bit lost, the qualities I hold closest to my heart are who I am. These are what I want to bring forth into the world.

Treat yourself with Respect (Rosen)

Whenever we allow ourselves to wallow in negativity in any form...

> self-pity, blaming, whining, complaining, excuses, self-deprecation,

> reacting defensively, etc,

...we are treating ourselves with disrespect.

Think about these two key ideas for a minute:

We don't like it when someone else treats us with disrespect or treats us unkindly.

Why do we allow ourselves to do it on a regular basis to ourselves?

Know yourself and respect the person you are at your core and you will find ways every day to help to bring that person to the fore when you interact with others.

Get support, too

When life gets tough, get help. There is nothing better for our own self-worth than the support of others (except perhaps, helping support others, see below). Do something for yourself when life is 'down' on you. Get the help of those who care about you and take some time for yourself when you need it.

> And for that extra self-boost – find someone who needs some help. It is the best medicine I know of, because when you see them smile, you will start smiling, too.

Questions and Ideas for Contemplation

A good exercise is to take a 'typical' encounter you have with your difficult boss and reflect on the negative self-talk that begins as part of that interaction and lasts far beyond it. What are you saying to yourself and how do you feel? Write all this down, as it can be very cathartic. You will have something concrete to look at to show you how you respond to these types of situations.

After you have done this, brainstorm and write down more positive ways you could support yourself throughout this type of difficult situation. If you do this a few times, you will find yourself quite capable of doing it in even difficult, interactions. You will find the dynamics of those encounters will change dramatically for the better in a very short time. (see also Part II of this book)

Add the dialogue of those who love you to your internal dialogue. Consider your parents, best friend, favorite uncle or teacher... whatever they might say to comfort you in this situation – say it to yourself.

Chapter 4

SELF-CONFIDENCE

How confident are you in your daily dealings with your difficult boss?

If you feel confident, then how do you manifest that in your interactions with him/her?

If you don't feel confident, what will it take to learn to be more self-positive and assertive?

Self-Confidence leads to Assertive Behavior

The questions above set the stage for understanding and working with your own behaviors/approach to others through positive self-worth.

HOW you deal with your boss says a great deal about whether you feel truly confident in yourself and your approach, or whether you are substituting ego-driven behavior because you are actually coming from a stance of negative self-worth.

Aggressive behavior, though it appears to be self-confident, generally is rooted in feelings of inadequacy and poor self-worth. The ego takes over and drives us to continually prove who we are, that we are in control, that we 'have what it takes,' etc.

There is no need to push, bully, or otherwise force people into your way of thinking/doing things IF you are confident about what you say, and confident in the way you represent yourself and your ideas.

Passive-Aggressive behaviors, in which a person will use manipulation and behind-the-back techniques to get their way, is based in a fundamental lack of confidence and in negative self-esteem. Passive-aggressive personalities find less direct means to get their way. They don't resort to aggressive, in-your-face behaviors because they have found that they are more successful with manipulating others through more indirect and often devious methods: gossiping, talking behind people's backs, working to get their way by convincing others to vote/work against you, etc.

Passive people rarely appear self-confident, often staying out of the mainstream of office politics and hullabaloo by just not being involved. They may have even perfected the 'be there, do nothing' technique of staying out of trouble, i.e. "If I don't do or say anything, no one can blame me for it."

Your approach makes a major difference to your success

> Carry yourself with confidence; bullies respect (personal) power and strength. (Lubit)

It is very common for employees to feel overshadowed by a powerful authority figure. Some bosses can be extremely demanding, domineering, aggressive, and critical. Often people react to these types of behaviors passively or passive-aggressively. Office dynamics with an aggressive boss at the fore may include a great deal of grumbling, complaining, blaming (finger-pointing), whining, and general negativity, i.e. very typical passive-aggressive behaviors. And these behaviors often are not aimed directly at the perpetrator.

It is also common to react to this forceful type of personality non-aggressively. People may simply avoid conflict and interactions like the plague. Depression sets in. they become low-achievers, and there is very little interest or enjoyment in work (and often life) anymore.

Learn Assertiveness

Most of us have used a wide range of behaviors throughout our lives in dealing with difficult others. The key to being successful with the many different, and difficult, types of bosses that you can work for is to develop positive, assertive behaviors from a solid sense of self.

Assertive people know their limits, and the limits of others. They consider how what they think, do, and say impacts others and themselves (see Lubit, Emotional Intelligence – personal and social competence, pp. 4-5)

Aggressive and Passive-Aggressive people tend to exceed acceptable human limits when interacting with others. We often feel uncomfortable, anxious, and ill-at-ease in their presence.

We CAN change if we tend to be more aggressive, passive-aggressive, or passive in our interactions with authority figures. We can learn to take a positive, self-affirming stance even with really difficult people. When we begin to make these changes in our own approach, it almost always effectively changes the dynamics of our interactions with others – difficult or not.

How can you learn assertiveness?

Changing our regular patterns of behavior, how we interact with others, is not easy. However, as Nike's commercial has stated, you can make an effort to "Just Do It."

One way to approach developing more positive interaction patterns for ourselves IS to make a commitment to...

JUST DO IT!

You have already learned two of the Keys to developing positive, assertive behavior: Self-Awareness, and Self-Worth. The next step is to decide [right now would be a great time!] to...

make a commitment to change.

If you use typical 'fight and flight' behaviors in dealing with your boss, there are better choices:

> 'Fight' behaviors tend to be aggressive (and can be passive-aggressive), where we push back and resist our difficult boss' behavior. The problem with these types of responses is that bosses have long memories, and they usually do not like to be crossed. It is fairly common to end up in more hot water than when you started.

> 'Flight' behaviors are avoidance-based behaviors. You may flinch, back away, apologize, not respond, or use a variety of actions to get out of the way. While these behaviors may not get you in further trouble, they also rarely get you anywhere. And they often cause personal concerns – depression, illness, unhappiness, etc.

Make a different commitment now

Throughout this book, we will discuss how to use assertive, positive behaviors to work successfully with your boss. It <u>can</u> be done, even with really difficult bosses. Stay the course; be willing to try some of these techniques out. You might be very surprised at how well they work. Even bullies and domineering, aggressive bosses tend to respond more positively and respectfully to positive, assertive behaviors.

Our approach

I was once asked at a presentation whether it was possible to 'be right' and 'be kind' at the same time. My response was "It is always possible to be positive in working with another person," and then I added, "...regardless of how they are acting."

We believe in a positive, self-confident approach, based around self-examination and a solid sense of self. This can be learned, and it will be the focus of much of the rest of this book.

You Decide

When you interact with others, it is always within your power to decide how **you** will act. Being assertive means taking a firm, positive approach as you make behavioral decisions that are best for you and for others. It is important to keep in mind that what you do and say, and how you do and say it, can make a difference not only to you, to your boss, but also to fellow coworkers as well. Interactions are always at the very least a two-way street and often they are much more far-reaching than that.

Be Yourself

You can and should stand up for who you are and what you believe. The key idea here is that you don't have to do it defensively or aggressively. There are better ways -- ways that don't escalate encounters or create more angst for everyone.

Always keep in mind the important key idea that bosses typically have some type of power/rank over us. Learning to be positive and assertive is much better than reacting negatively, defensively, or aggressively.

Questions and Ideas for Contemplation

Consider the main ways in which you interact with and react to your boss:

> Are you aggressive? (defensive, fight back, get angry)

> Are you more passive-aggressive? (blame, complain, gossip to your coworkers)

> Are you more passive? (avoid, internalize, go into a 'shell')

Whatever way you tend to react, feel, interact, you can make changes that lead to a more in-control, assertive approach. The first step is to envision a more assertive, positive you in a typical interaction with your boss. Go through a typical boss scenario again and again in your head and try to find ways to be firm, self-affirming, and positive instead of making the same choices you have always made, i.e. choosing the way you might normally react.

You will receive many other suggestions, ideas, and examples of a positive, assertive approach throughout this book. As your knowledge and skill-base expand, come back to this type of exercise. Think about how more positive interactions with your boss can go. This type of inner practice can be very useful and lead to major changes in how you approach and interact with authority figures.

Chapter 5

SELF-CONTROL

"Control Yourself" (Cicero)

"To be great is not to be placed above humanity, ruling others; but to stand above the partialities and futilities of uniformed desire and to rule One's self." (Spinoza)

Self-Control grows naturally from Positive Self-worth and Self-Confidence

If you review the chapters on self-worth and self-confidence you will note upon rereading that there is much already written about self-control.

Reaction versus controlled Response

When we are negatively impacted by a difficult person (or situation), we tend to REACT, often negatively, to their demeanor and way of communicating. Not only is this natural, it is often fore-ordained by two key concepts:

> Your past will help dictate how you react – you have learned patterns of behavior built from many years of interpersonal experiences.

> Difficult people, consciously or sub-consciously, learn very quickly to play upon your patterns of reacting to them. It is to their advantage to do so, because they gain the upper hand when you lose control.

Hot Buttons

We all have 'buttons' that difficult people are experts at pushing and it doesn't take them very long to figure out what they are. The key point is that we don't have to let them gain control by their various tactics. We always have more positive, self-affirming choices we can make.

"What is the level of your emotionality?" (Bramsom)

It is not 'bad' to react emotionally to negativity. It is normal. What is 'bad' or negative is allowing this negativity to permeate our day, and our life. By paying attention to how we feel and what we are thinking about, we can control where this 'stuff' eventually ends up – as part of our pile of negativity, remorse, anguish, revenge, etc., that sits with us and impacts our life from this day forth, or as something we deal with immediately by examining it and making life-affirming choices instead.

More powerful, yet, is the knowledge that as we work on and deal with the negativity that impacts us on a day-to-day basis, we are also beginning to deal with the negativity we have stored up in the past. Deep rooted emotions – fear, anger, etc., impact how we react to and interact with others. Make positive LIFE choices for yourself and for your loved ones by learning to deal with negativity as it arises. The rest of this book will offer many ideas that will help you make better choices for yourself and for others.

You choose to be a victim of a difficult person

Our reaction/response is always a choice. We can choose to give over control to another person by reacting to their negativity and let them, in a sense, dictate our thoughts and feelings, or we can be assertive, positive, and make controlled responses instead.

Surprisingly it is not unusual for a difficult person to stop being difficult when we make wiser choices for ourselves. When we are in-control, they (even authority figures) can't control who we are, how we feel, and what we do. Yes, they can still negatively impact our life and our work, but the chances are very good that our assertiveness and positivity will change our interaction with them for the better. [See Part II of this book for many examples.] And even if they remain a jerk, we can have a much more enhanced and positive work environment in spite of their negativity and in spite of the bad choices **they** make.

Don't React -- Respond

Reacting to something implies we are not **in control**. If someone hits your knee in the right place with a small rubber hammer, you will have a 'knee-jerk reaction'. Just the same, if some $X#*G#@ driver screeches past you and gives you 'the finger,' when you are already going five miles over the speed limit on a two-lane road with a double yellow line, your typical reaction might be to immediately feel angry, upset, and perhaps give him 'the finger' back.

Sound familiar?

Difficult people learn very quickly how to get people to respond to their way of doing things. It helps make them feel powerful, in-control, and less inferior.

IMPORTANT POINT: most difficult behavior is the result of inferiority feelings and negative self-worth by the perpetrator.

Fear is at the root of difficult behavior. Fear is at the root of all negative affect. (Perkins)

As a long-time pursuer of knowledge and understanding about difficult people, I would probably say **ALL** difficult behavior is the result of internal negative feelings.

A domineering, aggressive person may not appear fearful, but it is most likely what is driving their behavior. They substitute bravado and negativity for their feelings of inadequacy. I have known a number of difficult people whose self-worth and hence behavior was predicated by having someone to put-down. This is actually a fairly common behavior pattern – by criticizing and debasing others, they avoid their own short-comings and raise themselves up in their own eyes. (See Chapters 19 and 20 on "Aggressive Bosses" and "Domineering Bosses.")

Catch yourself before you React

"What you do after something negative happens to you is *your* decision, not the other person's." (Roberta Cava)

Self-observation gives us the opportunity to catch our thoughts and feelings before we simply react to negative behavior from another person. In the instance it takes us to say, "Steve is really getting me uptight (upset, angry, depressed, etc.), we can say to ourselves, "I don't want to feel this way; what choices do I have?"

And it does only take an instant – especially if you practice this until it becomes a habit.

"Never put your mouth in drive while your brain is in neutral."

How does this change things?

Observing your thoughts and feelings doesn't necessarily, especially initially, change how you think or what you are feeling. It is actually important for you to acknowledge and let yourself feel the way you would normally feel. This is who you are at this moment in time, and that is okay.

What it does do is allow you time to contemplate, however briefly, those thoughts and emotions, and to observe what your typical reaction might be to this negative behavior impacting you. Then you do have the space and opportunity to make a RESPONSE (you maintain control), instead of simply reacting.

> I have practiced this technique for many years now and at first it was difficult not to just go ahead and use my normal defense, reaction mechanisms. What was easy to accomplish fairly quickly was the ability to see that I could make other choices. Now, I have even reached the point where some behaviors that would have really set me off in the past, don't affect me, because I know it is not my 'stuff.' It is the other person's negativity and lack of control.

As you develop this of self-observation technique, stopping automatic reactions, and choosing more positive responses, you will find that your interactions with 'difficult' people become much more manageable and you will also find that you have far fewer difficult people in your life. [See end of Chapter for another perspective on how to view this.]

Or is it that you don't see them as being so difficult anymore?

Or perhaps, that you just know how to deal with them so much better?

Yes, there are Jerks in the world

If you take the example I gave above about the person who gave the finger on the road, you can't find much of an explanation for such negative behavior other than that they are just being a royal jerk. At least they certainly were for that moment in time.

However, it is always a matter of perspective. [See the Chapters to follow on "Kindness" and "Positivity."] Maybe this guy just lost his job and he is angry at the world. This doesn't forgive his behavior, but it does help explain why 'you got in his way.'

We always have the choice of maintaining our control despite what someone else is doing, even when what they are doing is purposefully negative. Remember, though, that most difficult people have no conception about how negatively they come across to others. This goes for REALLY difficult people, too.

Questions and Ideas for Contemplation

Choosing between a REACTION to circumstance versus a controlled RESPONSE **is** a big deal. It is often equivalent to choosing negativity or positivity. Below is an excerpt from one of my books: *Understanding and Working with Difficult People*. This delineates this process from a different perspective. It is a method designed by Dr. John McQuaid, and used in therapy manuals at the VA Medical Center in San Diego. [Brown, S, McQuaid, J., Granholm, E., Koob, J., Roepke, S. *Group Therapy Manual for Cognitive-Behavioral Social Skills Training (CBSST) for Older Persons with Schizophrenia*; Brown, S, McQuaid, J., Granholm, E., Laumakis, M., Koob, J., *Group Therapy Manual for Twelve-Step Facilitation Treatment of Substance Dependence*, 1999-2000.]

Staying in control of you

In the course of my writing several manuals for drug and alcohol group therapy, Dr. John McQuaid introduced me to something he had written for use with the patients. I had also pursued similar reasoning as his in my book, *A Perfect Day: Guide for a Better Life*. When I became familiar with it, I liked Dr. McQuaid's approach a lot. As with many good ideas this one is simple and easy to remember:

Catch It

Check It

Change It

While the concept is not new, the 3 Cs idea makes it easy to remember.

Paying Attention equals "Catch it"

The first step in gaining and maintaining self-control in a difficult situation is to **Catch** yourself. By paying attention to your emotions, what you are thinking, and the reaction you are about to have (action you will take), you set yourself up for making a choice.

Choices...

are everything in difficult situations. Rather than buying into the other person's mania or difficulty and immediately reacting, you can now be who you want to be, who you choose to be. You make the choices. The other person does not control you by dragging you into their emotionality.

Check it

While this may seem like the obvious next step, it is not always so clear cut. You want everything about this difficult situation you find yourself in to be very clear. **Checking it** helps you set up making different choices than you would normally make.

Take a close look at your feelings, your thoughts, and your soon to be reaction. Is this really how you want to feel, think, and react?

The bomb didn't go off?

The simple act of checking these inner workings of your mind and body does a very important thing. It sets up a pause in the proceedings. That pause means you are still in control. It will also, very likely, puzzle the heck out of the difficult person. He wants and is waiting for, the expected reaction from you. When you don't explode, the situation no longer fits the norm. Behaviors can and very likely will change as a result.

Change it

Now! you have the choice of redirecting yourself and the situation. As you will find out, this makes all the difference in the world in dealing with difficult people.

Remember:

> **Catch it**: are you paying attention to yourself?

> **Check it**: is this really how you want to be?

> **Change it**: make a different choice

It is important to pay attention to how the difficult person you are dealing with reacts to this new turn of events, too.

Try practicing **Catch it, Check it, Change it** in a variety of situations this week. They don't have to be difficult situations; see if you can get the hang of it. You might be surprised at how much control you suddenly have -- control of yourself and the choices you make.

Chapter 6

HONESTY

Is being honest really smart... when dealing with my boss?

The Truth

What is closer to your truth?

> That you want...

>> To be defensive, angry, upset, frustrated,

>> To blame and complain

>> To avoid, cower, hide from someone

>> To be depressed, unhappy, unfulfilled?

> Or would you rather...

>> Be your true self with everyone; following those values and qualities that deep down really define who you really are and who you want to bring to the fore every day.

You cannot really have it both ways.

Choose the truth that makes you happy and vibrant. Choose YOU!

But...

> My boss really treats me and everyone else terribly...

> She puts me down at every opportunity; I feel like I have been run over.

I never get any acknowledgement from him for what I do; if anything, my boss takes credit for my ideas and leaves me hanging.

And so on...

'Buts' are excuses. Personally, I don't want to live my life based on a bunch of excuses. I want to take responsibility for who I am and what impacts me, and then make a difference.

How?

There are ALWAYS neutral and positive ways in which you can deal with negativity. You can be honest with someone and still treat them kindly (see next chapter). The rest of this book will show you many ideas, skills, and tools that will help you make more positive choices, while still maintaining your fundamental values and beliefs.

First and Foremost

Make a commitment to be honest with yourself. This starts with being honest about who you want to be, recognizing who you are through self-awareness, and recognizing your thoughts and feelings as you deal with difficult issues and people in your life. When we can be truly honest with ourselves, we can say things like...

"Oops, that wasn't a very positive thought..."

"I'm getting angry here. I'm angry because..."

"I am tense and frustrated because of how Mr. Brown is treating me. What choices do I have to..."

"I feel terrible. How can I turn this around? What can I do?"

These statements all exhibit one very important factor besides honesty – ownership. When we make these types of 'I' statements to ourselves we are effectively saying, "This is MY life and I'm going to take charge (self-control) and make it better. I'm not going to let someone else dictate how I feel and what I do."

Insist on others being honest with you

This is a tough one to get our minds around perhaps, but it also works if we couple this commitment with Kindness (see next Chapter). There is no reason you can't let others know what you expect of them, especially when it comes to the fundamental values and the qualities in your own life.

Say it:

"Francis I really appreciate your being honest with me. It means a lot."

You can say this up front, or even post hoc, whether they have been completely honest or not. You are working to get your point across and to set the stage for further interactions.

"Alyce, when you are open and honest with me, even if the news is tough, I really appreciate it. It means we respect each other and can get through the tough stuff together."

"Bob, I want to learn from my mistakes, so please let me know if I screw up. I will listen and learn. Your honesty really makes a difference."

Important points:

People don't know what we value unless we tell them (and tell them, and tell them, and...)

People will listen, though it may take them time to change how they approach you, but if you are persistent, they will listen and they will change.

People tend to be the way we let them know we want them to be. They try to live up to our expectations.

There are always a few who take a great deal of effort to get them to come around, so be patient and keep at it. You always have choices you can make that are best for you (see also Chapter 24, "Really Difficult Bosses").

If someone has been and seems to be consistently dishonest, you can even challenge them without blaming and then let them know how you feel:

"Gina, I thought you told me last week that we were doing 'X'. Maybe I got it wrong, but I know we need to be on the same page with this, so could we sit down and be open about what you expect. I will take careful notes so I get it right. I appreciate your being forthright about this issue and taking the time for me to understand exactly what's what."

With this type of response, you are leaving this person with an out. (Believe me, it never pays to blame your boss!) You are also telling them that you appreciate an honest approach, and you are reinforcing that by taking notes. (Hint: It helps people be honest the next time around!) It also lets them know that you value accountability – theirs and yours.

Bramson in his book, *Coping with Difficult Bosses*, uses the phrase, "matter-of-fact honesty.' And follows this up with "your purpose is to stop disagreeable behavior, not punish or insult."

The more you work with turning negative thoughts and **reactions**, which are our common reactions to negativity from someone else, into neutral or positive thoughts and **actions**, the more it will become second nature. Think before you respond and you will find that you can become consistent at being honest <u>and</u> <u>kind</u> at the same time.

Honesty does not mean

Being disrespectful – there are always kind and compassionate ways to say things.

Telling your boss what you really think of him – while you may be tempted – it NEVER helps!

Pointing out to your boss all the mistakes he/she makes

Telling others what you really think of your boss and pointing out to others the mistakes he/she makes.

Complaining, whining, and otherwise wallowing in negativity –

Remember Negativity NEVER helps.

In other words

Don't use Honesty as an excuse to be mean and negative, regardless of how your boss is and how he treats you and others.

Bosses are People, too

It may be hard to believe at times, but your ogre boss is actually a person with feelings (I know, I know, that may be a hard one to swallow sometimes), a real life, and even the potential to be human.

If you give them a chance, you may be very surprised at how they come around. Honesty is a BIG part of respect. Honesty and respect work both ways:

Be honest; also, expect others to treat you honestly.

Be respectful; and others will very likely learn to respect you.

Questions and Ideas for Contemplation

Integrity is a word I have written a fair amount about because it has a great deal to do with good leadership. When we are 'in integrity' (Perkins), we CAN expect others to treat us the same way. And there is nothing demanding about that. It is an outgrowth of how we want to be and how we wish to be perceived and treated. When we act as if we deserve honesty, respect, and when we act with integrity, we act as though we expect the same courtesy from others. It may be surprising, but it may be all that you need to do to help turn around a person who treats you badly.

We will answer other in-depth questions related to being honest throughout this work. Think about some of the following scenarios. A boss who...

is consistently secretive, behind-the-back, or even blatantly dishonest.

says one thing to you and another thing to a colleague.

keeps everything from the team, hoarding information or just being uncommunicative.

says and does things in such a way that you and your colleagues have no real idea what is expected of you until the axe falls.

Just keep in mind that the old adage is very true, especially when dealing with authority figures, "Honesty is the best policy," or taken from the other side, "Dishonesty doesn't pay." It just doesn't.

A person with integrity is someone who can be counted on to do the right thing, even when no one is looking. Have you been tempted to 'not do the right thing' because you thought the boss would never find out? Don't give your boss a reason to be difficult!

Chapter 7

KINDNESS

"When you have a choice between being right and being kind, choose being kind." (Wayne Dyer)

Being kind is a choice we can make every day, many times a day.

Kindness is not just a wise choice; it is a choice that reaps manifold benefits for all those within reach, including yourself.

Being Kind

Every human being deserves kindness, especially the difficult ones.

We are all human beings and it is hard to say who or how a person got to be the way they are. Difficult people are hurting inside, whether they admit it or not. Their pain comes out in many forms, and it does hurt other people. But just imagine how that pain might change if one person, or several, or a bunch, were kind to them in the same day – makes you stop and think, doesn't it?

"Sometimes people are difficult because life is hard. Kindness is what they need from you more than anything else." (Rosen)

A Positive Perspective

The person you are dealing with may be having a bad day.

> We all have bad days, and it is nice when someone is kind to us.

The person we are dealing with may be having a bad week, month, year.

> We have all probably had a few of those, too.

The person we are dealing with may be having a bad/tough life.

We can even understand this, if we try.

Your choosing to be kind, may be the difference between a really bad day or helping them turn their day around and start afresh.

Your choosing to be kind, may be the difference between them having a bad week, month, or year or them having a chance to turn this difficult period in their life around and start down a new path.

Your choosing to be kind and compassionate, could even be the difference, that one needed difference, it might take to help them begin to turn their life around.

Yes, it is possible. How we approach our day-to-day work life and our interactions can make a difference, a BIG difference to someone else – and to ourselves.

Being Right versus Being Kind

Author's Note: Wayne Dyer's quote at the beginning of this Chapter is one of my favorites. I have been thinking about this 'dilemma' of Being Right versus Being Kind for as long as I have been writing about difficult people.

Often when we are face-to-face with a difficult person who is 1) obviously wrong and 2) extremely adamant about their position and 3) very negative, pushy, and domineering to boot, it is hard to see any way to be kind.

As I illustrated earlier, when I was asked at a presentation, "Is it possible to be kind and right at the same time?" I answered, "Yes," and gave the young man an example. However, that question stayed with me and after the presentation I pondered it for some time and realized I had only given a partial answer. I should have added,

"What is so important about being right?"

An Example

An example used earlier that most people have experienced at least once in their lifetime is when someone in a car cuts you off, is rude, etc. How do we typically react?

We get upset and angry. We grip the steering wheel and maybe swear at the guy either out loud or in our mind. We break into a sweat, feel flushed, and really feel like it would be great to hit something, and so on.

We may react negatively by honking our horn, speeding up and tailgating, and by giving the person the finger back, etc.

We may feel confused about why this person is acting this way and perhaps even guilty, though we have done nothing wrong, and not in any way 'asked' to be treated this way.

We begin to simmer and express outrage (to ourselves). This negativity pervades our life for the next few hours (typically) and may even last for a day or more. The bottom line is that it does affect us negatively and we are hard-pressed to not let it bother us.

These are all normal reactions; the key point to consider is what good does any negative reaction do us?

We are absolutely right. This person is most probably a jerk. He/she has treated us badly and certainly made a good stab at ruining our day. He/she deserves our wrath.

Choosing Kindness

Being right, most of the time hardly ever does anything, except feed our egos. It is not about honor, though people may think so. It is not about 'if we get to be right' we win something.

Think this scenario through carefully. What do you 'win' if you are right? Satisfaction? For/from whom? Even if you feel you have gained 'satisfaction' what does that mean? Does it make a difference? Really make a difference?

Unfortunately, having 'satisfaction' from someone is a long-antiquated notion. I cannot find any good reason for it other than to feed our egos.

Feed your self-worth instead by being the outstanding person you want to be.

IMPORTANT: On the rare occasions that being right does make a difference, there are always ways to be right positively and kindly. This is especially critical with bosses. Keep the POWER thing in mind when dealing with authority figures. Bosses like to, and often need to, be right – to feed their own egos. [We will provide you with more examples of 'rightness' versus 'kindness' specifically related to bosses later on in this book.]

Positive Choices for You

Acknowledge your emotions. It is perfectly all right to do this, and it is best to go ahead and feel and observe how you react in difficult situations. When you do this, you deal with your anger, frustration, etc., immediately and don't 'stuff it' to be dredged up later.

> For example: It is okay to feel your anger, acknowledge your right to be angry, and to go with the flow of your emotions. Feel it, think about it, and then be done with it for the rest of this day AND for the rest of your life.

Then, choose not to react outwardly to this idiot. Tell yourself that:

> It doesn't matter in the grand scheme of things.

> This person may be having a very bad day.

> Your choice of not being negative is kind not only to the person who perpetrated this atrocity upon you, but it is also, importantly, **kind to yourself and everyone else you will interact with for the next few hours**.

> Being right, in this situation, isn't going to matter, except to your ego. What you want to take care of is your self-worth. Remember our self-worth is predicated by positive values and qualities, not negative ones.

Stop insisting on being right and grant the <u>honor</u> to someone else (Hoover) [My emphasis.]

There are many times that we have the opportunity to put our egos on hold and give our 'rightness' away to another person. In truth, we haven't really given anything up and as we learn to do this, it becomes easier and easier. We begin to see the value it has in our lives and the lives of others, because we were big enough to let these little petty things go.

"Can you feel good about yourself without having to feel superior to someone else?" (Rosen)

Bless the idiots in your life

Idiots, for all their negativity and concerns, might just be there to help us learn something (see Chapter 10). They probably can use all the positivity, kindness, and compassion you can come up with and then some. It is amazing how your kindness CAN make a difference, especially over time.

It is okay to be kind to your boss

Bosses are human (if you have doubts, keep reading). They need and deserve to be treated as we all wish to be treated. It is wise, as long as you are not obsequious about it, to treat bosses kindly and compassionately, regardless of how obnoxious, negative, domineering, aggressive, etc., they are.

How to be kind to your boss

There will be a great deal more written about this key idea throughout this text (see next Chapter "Positivity;" Chapter 9, "Knowing Your Boss;" and Chapter 13, "Little Things you can do right now to make a BIG Difference," etc.) however, here are a several early examples:

Make kindness a part of their (and your) day.

Write a short memo to your boss first thing in the morning:

> Bob,
>
> I just wanted to let you know I am moving steadily ahead with the Jones' contract. I should have all the data from Steve by Tuesday and a first draft done Thursday. If you would like to see the early drafts, let me know. I will keep you posted if anything changes.
>
> Have a great day, Joe

There are a number of key ideas illustrated by this memo:

> It is always wise to keep in contact with your boss. A brief memo is a very good idea, particularly if you don't get to see your boss that much. It is a good idea anyway.
>
> BRIEF and to the point are crucial. This should be something he/she can read in a few seconds and delete. You made contact, you were nice. He will probably, in one sense, ignore this memo like he ignores much of what crosses his desk, but he will, somewhere in his consciousness remember that you are:
>
> On top of things; proactive

Keeping him up to date (information sharing is critical to happy bosses)

Being nice to boot, though he may not specifically remember what you said that was nice.

You can actually do this every day; or every other day. Be sure to change your 'kind' expressions, don't get into a rut:

"It looks like it is going to be a great day!"

"Hope the wife and kids are doing well."

"Good luck with Frick group meeting today."

And so forth

Another great way to be kind on a regular basis is to make a sincere effort to end every interaction with your boss on a kind/positive note:

Sincere compliments are great

Saying 'Thanks' (One of those great tools/skills we tend to forget about.)

A simple kind word or phrase

You will come up with many the more you do this.

Here is another key point

"Allowing someone else to be right doesn't make you wrong." (Hoover)

This statement is very true. In the 'car cuts-you-off' scenario above, you don't come out 'wrong,' just because you insist on not 'being right.'

Think about this concept for a moment. Being right is often about letting the other person know they were wrong to do what they did. Sometimes it IS important to do this kindly; many times, it is much better to let this tension and upset go. Being right won't help you feel better, and it often very effectively exacerbates the situation.

Many interactions with people are this way. How we react is predicated by whether or not our egos are involved, and whether we need to be right, not whether we actually need to have our ideas/actions validated.

Even when there is a need to be right, to come out of an interaction with our ideas considered and accepted, there are many ways to make that happen kindly and positively. [Keep reading – Chapters 14, 15, and 16 on Communications discuss many ideas, skills, and tools relevant to this important point.]

Kindness is so much better

Choosing kindness instead of 'rightness' is not necessarily easy.

Sometimes we have to stop ourselves in difficult situations and ask:

> This is really upsetting me; do I need to be 'right' here?

> How can I choose kindness instead?

> What can I do to turn this negativity around?

The truth is that the more we think about and practice kindness, the better we feel, the better days we will have, and maybe most importantly, the days will be better for all the people we interact with.

Hoover in his book *How to Work for an Idiot* asks a very good question:

"If it's your boss or someone higher on the corporate

food chain, what do you think you are going to gain

by convincing her she is wrong?"

It is a question worth thinking about.

Compassion

Compassion is a great word to couple with Kindness. It adds just that bit extra that says we are making an effort to consider the concerns and difficulties that this difficult person we are working with is having with their life. Mark Rosen is his wonderful book, *Thank You for Being Such a Pain,* perhaps says it best:

"Look with compassion at the suffering that must invariably lie at the root of problem behaviors."

Questions and Ideas for Contemplation

Think of a recent encounter with your difficult boss and see if you can pick out the dynamics related to your feelings. Was part of this about the need to feel like you were right, heard, accepted, appreciated, etc? Can you separate your feelings in such a way as to acknowledge what you think you needed and what you actually needed?

Can you find ways to see this whole interaction in a more positive, kind way? Can you envision how taking a different approach can change the whole way this progresses?

Reworking through difficult situations you have had is a great way to practice ideas and techniques discussed in this book. More than anything else, it keys you into thinking about things the next time you have to work closely with this difficult individual. Your dynamics will change, and so will theirs.

Chapter 8

POSITIVITY

"We choose our attitude just as we choose

what to wear each day." (Perkins)

"If you keep a green bough in your heart,

the singing bird will come." (Old Chinese Proverb)

There is Negativity, why not Positivity?

Negativity breeds Negativity

Positivity breeds Positivity

Choose Wisely!

This is one of our favorite sayings at Metacoach LLC and Difficultpeople.org. It says a great deal in a limited space and it covers one of the most important keys to being successful with a difficult boss. Another way to put this is:

Negativity doesn't help.

It just doesn't.

You may have every right to be angry, frustrated, to blame your very difficult boss, to yell, scream, swear, to anyone who will listen about how badly you have been/are being treated, etc.

Yes, you can:

Complain

Whine

Gossip

Blame/Point your finger

Rant and Rave to your boss or to anyone who will listen

File a lawsuit

Explain to your boss what an idiot he is

Tell your boss that he is wrong

But the truth is, odds on, the person you are going to hurt the most is YOU (and very likely your reputation.)

There are better ways, much better ways

> "You can't change bad bosses, but you can change the way you approach and deal with them, which can change how you feel about yourself, and life in general." (Hoover)

One of the most important keys to being more positive throughout your work life is to take a close look at how you interact with others on a regular basis. This takes courage.

> Many years ago, I took a hard look at myself and decided something had to change. I wasn't very happy with my life, especially my work life. One of the bravest things I have ever done in my life was to ask a trusted colleague how I came across to others. I asked her to be open and honest with me. I was somewhat prepared, but to say the least I was shocked by what she told me and I know she made every effort to be kind.

> That is when I decided it was time to turn my life around. I decided that the negativity I had bought into and had begun to wallow in was not **who I wanted to be**. What I wanted to be was kind, compassionate, and positive. In the process, I learned how important it was for me to be honest about who I wanted to be as a person and also honest with myself about how other people perceived me as a person.

If you...

> Are not happy at work

Are not happy with your life

Find yourself complaining about a lot of things

Find yourself blaming others, your boss, your company for things that happen regardless of whose 'fault' it is

Find yourself blaming 'them' for your lot in life

Worry a lot

Are depressed, frustrated; feeling helpless, guilty, unappreciated

Spend a great deal of time gossiping negatively in and about work, whining...

And so on.

You are creating, at least during these times, an aura of negativity that people WILL pick up on. You won't know this unless you are willing to honestly observe your interactions with others and the world in general. And if you really want to see yourself as others see you, get the courage up to ask a trusted friend or colleague. You may be very surprised at what you find out.

Take responsibility for your life and work

Things don't always go right for me. I'm not always happy and I don't always get my way. I don't have everything I think I want. I don't always feel good emotionally, physically, mentally, or spiritually. I have good days and bad days just like everyone else.

The KEY difference between who I was twenty years ago and today is that I don't put the onus on -- other people, the world, 'them,' or some authority figure or power figure -- for my concerns. Instead I ask myself, what do I need to do to make this different. I take responsibility for my life. That choice has changed my life for the better because I am happier than I ever was before.

Take responsibility for being positive in your life and work

From this point on YOU can make a choice to be more positive, proactively positive, about your life. You will enjoy your life much more and feel more positive and in-control of how you get through your work and life as a result.

I have told the following little story a number of times in workshops and several times in my books, but it is well worth reiterating briefly here:

> I used to frequent a local grocery store when I lived in Oklahoma. I went there for two main reasons – it was close to my house, and, more importantly, I often ran into a particular checkout clerk. She was a grandmotherly type and as outgoing and boisterously friendly as anyone I have ever known. Her positivity was literally infectious. I don't think anyone could be grumpy or mean around this lady. She 'made my day' so many times that one day when I went through her line, I picked up a bouquet of flowers, paid for them, and handed them to her as a way of saying 'thanks for being who you are.' She cried; we hugged. With a small positive gesture, I made her day and mine.

> The truth is – we have this power within us every day.

We always have the power

> I am not a naturally outgoing, bubbly personality, but I make an effort every time I am with others to be kind and to be positive, even if I am feeling shy and introverted. When we do this on a regular basis, pervasively, it is hard for even really negative people to be and stay grumpy.

You may think, 'there is no hope for my boss.' But I can assure you that almost every situation I have ever seen, coached, and been involved with had the potential to be turned around by some sincere kindness, compassion, and positivity.

Positivity is something we can practice

Try it for a week.

> I used to teach an "Introduction to College Success" course and one of the projects I gave to students was to have them go out and purposefully say five kind things to people before the next class session and to take notes on their reactions. Several of the people they interacted with had to be strangers.

> The results were always amazing. Everyone came back telling me how much it meant to the people they had been kind to.

> It really can be that simple.

Sometimes all your difficult person/boss needs is a little appreciation and kindness themselves. It may take a while, but if you keep at it, I can virtually guarantee success.

Important: Be aware that it is possible, even likely, that your positivity and magnanimous nature may not be met by your boss. (Bramson) At least not right away, but there is always the possibility that over time your positive attitude WILL rub off and that things will improve over the long haul.

Be positive for you

"Too often, we let others control how we feel about ourselves. We allow them to give us bad or good days."

(Cava, *Dealing with Difficult People*)

In my book, *A Perfect Day: Guide for a Better Life*, I recommend that we start each day when we wake and end each day just before we drift off, with positive thoughts. This can be simply a few minutes we take envisioning positive thoughts as we lay in bed. We can choose positivity instead of worrying, which is more typical during these quiet moments.

Even when we are in the midst of a bad day or just got out of a negative encounter, we can help ourselves by telling ourselves that the rest of the day will be better. (Cava, *Dealing with Difficult People...*) You have the power to choose how you will think and feel THIS minute. As often as possible, make choices that free you to live as happily and positively as feasible.

There are many ways we can energize the positivity in our day by taking care of ourselves and by being open to treating ourselves, as well as through teaching others as kindly and positively as possible. (see also Chapter 11, "Taking Care of Yourself")

Positivity has a ripple effect. We have opportunities every day to spread good feelings and ideas around. Consistently drop the right seed in the soil and you will see it grow.

What are you wearing today?

We choose our **attitude** just as we choose what to wear each day.

What are you wearing today?

How are you affecting others?

How are you 'infecting' others?

What do you want other people, especially your difficult boss, to see you wearing?

Choose wisely.

Questions and Ideas for Contemplation

Think of ways, without being overly sentimental, that you can be positive at work, with your coworkers, and with your boss. As you get into the swing of things, you will begin to notice changes. Changes in the way other people react and interact with you. Changes in the way people/your boss perceive you. It is so much better than any form of negativity.

Chapter 9

KNOWING YOUR BOSS

"You can only influence others when you see them as they are, not as you wish they were…" Formulate "a picture of how the world must look to them, as distorted as that view may seem…. understanding does not imply approval, acceptance, or liking."

(Bramson)

He is more than his difficult behavior

When we work for someone who seems to be a consistent pain-in-the-neck, it is difficult to get beyond the presenting behaviors he manifests throughout his interactions with others. The truth is even really difficult authority figures have a human side. When we open ourselves up to that understanding, we have a chance of finding it and helping that person bring it to the fore.

"Learn to separate the individual from the difficulty

you associate with him." (Perkins)

Know 'Why?'

When we can stand back and ask ourselves, "Why is he/she manifesting these types of difficult behaviors?" we can begin to understand the person. This opens up the possibility for us to accept and understand the feelings of the person we are working with. (Bramson)

There are many reasons a boss could be difficult and while it might be helpful to understand some of his past and be able to explore the psychological foundation for his eccentricities and difficult behaviors, unless you have a graduate degree in psychology or counseling it is probably better to stick with developing a sense of your boss' needs, wants, and desires – his intent.

A word of caution: there are a number of books in the difficult people literature that focus on labeling difficult people through a variety of means:

Descriptive labels: Cowardly Lions; Slippery Snakes; Exploding Bombs, etc.

Psychologically-based labels, (using the *DSM-IV, Diagnostic and Statistical Manual of Mental Disorders* of the American Psychiatric Association): Borderline Personality Disorder, Antisocial, Paranoid, etc.

Please Note: I sincerely believe that labels of any kind, while they can be helpful in a broad sense, are limiting. They make us focus on a generic concept and not on the individual or the specific behavior. Everyone IS different and we all manifest our eccentricities/differences in personal ways. In addition, labeling using psychiatric foundations is very difficult and not an exact science, it should never be used by those who don't have extensive study and experience in this area, e.g. while most of us could be 'labeled' paranoid at times (i.e. we all have things we fear), the vast majority of us are not paranoid, nor paranoid-schizoid personalities.

Intent

Brinkman and Kirschner in their book, *Dealing with People You Can't Stand,* have an excellent section on **Intent**, which focuses on behavior. Much of what follows in this section jumps off from their unique perspective.

When we humans interact, especially at work, we generally intend some outcome or purpose to the interaction. People want to

Get it done

Get it right

Get along

Get appreciated

Be cared for (Koob)

For example:

An exploding boss' intent may be to 'get something right'.

A boss who is trying to be everyone's best buddy may need to 'get along' and/or 'be appreciated.'

A pushy, domineering boss may want you to 'get things done.'

53

And so on.

I added 'cared for' to Brinkman and Kirschner's list of four 'Intents' above, because I also firmly believe that we all want to be cared for and cared about, even at work.

We can go a long way toward understanding our bosses and being able to work with them successfully by paying attention to them and making an effort to appease their intent:

If I have a 'get it right,' nit-picking, hyper-critical boss, I want to pay a good bit of attention to getting the things right that I do for him/her.

If I have a 'get it done' boss, I want to be sure I make all deadlines and to keep projects moving ahead.

Generally speaking, we all like to 'get along,' though you might not think so by the negativity some people regularly exhibit. We all appreciate 'being appreciated,' and it is nice when people care for who we are and what is important to us.

It is wise and helpful to let your boss know you are on the same page as they are and understand what is important to them:

"Beth, I appreciate your wanting to get this project done on time. I just wanted to let you know I am on top of it and I will let you know immediately if there are any time constraints."

"Greg, I have worked through this paper several times and it seems to be in tip-top shape. Fred has been through it, too. However, we know you like things to be perfect, so we hope you will go through it piecemeal and make sure we caught everything."

"Tom, I think we have got all the data set up into the types of grafts you prefer. Let me know if there is anything you would like adjusted."

It doesn't hurt to let them know you know, OFTEN!

Needs, Wants, and Desires

Understanding your boss and his/her needs goes beyond knowing what their intent is. Often making an effort to understand who they are addresses the concerns that may be behind their difficult behavior (e.g. needing to be cared for, paid attention to). You can be fairly well assured that a regularly difficult person is hurting inside:

Dealing with/reacting to low self-esteem, feelings of inferiority

Not feeling appreciated, recognized, cared for

Fear of 'being found out,' i.e. they aren't competent, knowledgeable, perfect, etc.

Feeling isolated, left out, unconnected

Anxious about how they appear to you, others, the team, upper management

Wanting to be in-control, but feeling anything but

Needing to be the center of attention (recognized/part-of)

The specifics are manifold, but the solution is not as difficult as you may think.

"Nobody knows the troubles They have seen." (Rosen)

They may not just be having a bad day, but having a bad life.

Appreciation, Recognition, Being a part of

Our needs as an employee, which is what the vast majority of us base our happiness and comfort upon at work, are centered in **how we feel** – not in our salary, benefits, promotions, or other tangibles. We want to be appreciated and recognized for who we are, what we do, and to be a part of 'the team,' the group, the organization.

Guess what? Bosses feel the same way.

Being appreciative of a boss who is on a rampage day in and day out may be the furthest thing from your mind. But if you can find ways to let her know you appreciate her; you will probably find that she wasn't such an ogre after all. Find ways to appreciate and recognize her – to make her a part of the team. Let her know you appreciate her knowledge, her strengths, whatever you can find about her behavior that is a plus. Recognize her when she does do positive, constructive things for you and/or your team, and you will find she begins to seem like a 'regular person.'

I have seen this many times in working with managers and executives. The persona they seem to have in relationship to their employees is so dramatic and standoffish that they push people away and even alienate them. But if you talk with them on a personal level, you find that they care very much about how they are perceived, and wish they could change everyone's perception of them.

You are probably not going to have that kind of in-depth personal discussion with your boss. But what you can do is to make an effort daily to treat them with respect, care, appreciation, etc.

"The secret to getting along well with other people *is to find their need and to be willing to fill it.*" (Littauer)

Respect

Respect is a key concept at work. It is something that we appreciate receiving from our colleagues, our employees, and from our boss. Keep this key concept in mind any time you deal with your boss. Respect must start somewhere, with someone. You can be the catalyst that starts the ball rolling in your office.

Yes, it would be great if your boss would respect you, but if he doesn't, then you need to set the stage by being willing to be respectful of everyone you work with, AND, very importantly, making sure that you respect yourself. You show respect for yourself by valuing yourself, being assertive and confident, and by maintaining self-control. You show respect to others in the same way. Add some kindness and compassion and you can change the world about you.

> At times, perhaps far too often, we lose sight of the important fact that there is something very fundamental that we all share. When we really think about it, even when we try hard to put our fingers on what it really is, it is never easy to describe. What makes us human? What is our humanity?

> But when we do make that effort, we take a step higher on the ladder of what humanity is all about.

> Every time we say something negative about someone to another person, we are showing disrespect to both people. AND, in essence, we are not respecting ourselves at this point, either. (Koob, *Honoring Work and Life: 99 Words for Leaders to Live By*).

In essence

When you support your boss' self-esteem, his needs, you can quickly change the dynamics of your interactions with him – AND he will often change his interactions with all your team members as a result. It may not happen right away; some hurts go very deep (see Chapters 23 and 24). However, if you persist, the chances are very good your efforts will have an impact.

Some additional ideas

As we discuss more specifically the behaviors of difficult bosses in the second part of this book, we will talk about other positive things you can do to help change the dynamics of a tense relationship. Here are a few others to contemplate:

> Show acceptance and understanding of the feelings of the person you are talking with. (Cava)

> Treat your boss like you would want him to be. Set the stage by showing him through your own actions and words, how you would like him to treat you. Treat him how you would like to be treated if you were the boss.

> Humanize your relationship – call him/her by name (unless they specifically request otherwise); be personal and accepting; recognize their knowledge and their worth. (Bramson)

> Observe how your boss does things – people like to work in predictable ways/routines, knowing this can help you work with someone on their turf. (Toporov; Koob)

> Agree on ground rules for working together, predicated strongly by their intent and needs. In other words, talk it out; don't leave these kinds of things to chance. (Osbourne)

> Never make excuses; take responsibility. (Toporov)

Questions and Ideas for Contemplation

Difficult people can be extremely exasperating, but they are people – people who will respond to kindness, positivity, acknowledgment, appreciation, and understanding. When you make the effort, they will very likely notice.

There are always considerations when deciding how you will make adjustments to your behavior in order to hopefully effect positive change in someone else. Slow and judicious change may be better than a sudden complete reversal of your behavior patterns. Though positive change is rarely perceived as negative, it could perhaps be seen as a bit odd at first. Count on your own insight and your understanding of the other person. Pay attention to the dynamics in the office as you make changes. Stay alert and flexible, and take care of yourself as you reinforce the specific behavioral changes you are trying to make.

Never forget that POWER thing. Be smart; be safe.

Chapter 10

LEARNING

"Learning how to transform enmity is

one of our most important life lessons." (Mark Rosen)

"I try to remember that everything that irritates us about others can lead us to an understanding of ourselves." (Ursula Markham)

I have been a teacher as far back as I can remember – my siblings and I used to play school, and I had my first violin student when I was eleven. Learning/education is as much a part of me as breathing. I love to learn, and to this day I still buy and read history books, how-to books, textbooks, do word games, etc. I see life as a huge school in which to learn.

One saying I had pinned to the bulletin board outside my office the whole time I taught college was, **"One's best Teacher is Himself."** It is a quote that says much about what is in this chapter. [I can't remember whether I originally said this or if it is a quote I found long ago. If so, the source is long forgotten. See later in this chapter for an updated version.]

"Life is a School and Difficult People are the Faculty" (Rosen)

This is a great way to perceive the difficult people and situations we encounter throughout our lives. If we can make the effort to bring this concept to mind when we find ourselves in a difficult spot, we can bring a far different and less negatively charged attitude to the situation.

Ask yourself, "What can this person teach me?" Or "What can I learn from this situation that I can take with me?"

Life's Difficulties are presented to us for us to Learn

Whether we look at life with a belief foundation that suggests that things happen for a reason or not, I have always found it interesting to consider the possibility that the difficult people and difficult situations that I encounter in life seem to keep coming back to bug me until I learn what is necessary to deal with them positively and successfully.

As an interesting sidelight to the work I have done over the past few years centered around "Understanding and Working with Difficult People," I now rarely encounter difficult people. Perhaps I have learned to deal with them better, or maybe I just don't encounter them anymore, or it could be I just don't see these types as difficult anymore. I have learned and my life is more positive as a result.

When we look at the world as a series of challenges, we face difficulties proactively rather than as a victim. This change of perspective allows us to maintain control of ourselves and of the situation. The dynamics of difficult situations are very different when we keep this idea in the forefront of our minds.

You will learn a lot about Yourself if you study Difficult People

There is a great deal written by a wide variety of authors, psychologists, and spiritual writers that centers around the idea that difficult people are holding a mirror up for us to look into, i.e. that the behaviors that we see as difficult in others are the very behaviors we need to consider in ourselves.

I have considered this concept from a wide variety of angles and I am not totally convinced 'Yea' or 'Nay' as to the validity of this perspective. However, I do believe that if we make an effort to understand difficult people, we will learn a lot about ourselves. I have also seen, in working with clients and through self-observation, that we do indeed sometimes react very strongly to behaviors that we could probably work on ourselves. This is particularly relevant to issues centered around poor self-image. People who are quite sensitive to certain types of criticism are often very critical of the very same types of things in other people.

I am not convinced that every difficult behavior I see in another person is directly relevant to my own behavior. However, it is true that if I see the behavior as difficult, that it is in some way pushing my buttons, and therefore, it offers me the opportunity and choice to learn something more from this type of behavior and this situation.

You can always ask yourself when someone is bugging you:

"What is this revealing about me?

And,

"What can I learn from this as a result?" (Markham)

Learn about Yourself

"Be curious about what the experience with a difficult person might teach you." (Perkins)

Any time you are in a difficult situation or encounter you have the opportunity to learn something. You can learn about others; you can learn about how the world wags, and perhaps even a little about what/who wags it. And you can learn about yourself – how you respond to the world, and what you can do about that.

It is fairly fascinating to step back in your mind during an encounter with someone and observe your emotions, thoughts, physical sensations, and your reactions; then to take it one step further and ask yourself, "Is this how I want to react to this?"

This process, if practiced, can give you a great deal of control of a situation through your own self-control. [See Chapter 5 – Catch it; Check it; Change it]

Your "...most powerful option for dealing with a difficult person is personal growth." (Rosen)

"No matter how miserable your situation, your solution starts in your head..." (Hoover)

Looking at difficulties as learning opportunities affords you the power to make changes and to find solutions. Difficult bosses can, and do, create major problems and concerns for us. We can fight back or run away from these problems, or we can get busy learning how to make the most of what we are dealing with through our own understanding and growth.

Learning has at its foundation the broad concept,

What can I Do?

There is a great deal you can do. Part of what you can do is finish reading this book, but long after this book and other educational opportunities are past, you can continue to teach yourself.

One's best teacher IS Oneself.

Questions and Ideas for Contemplation

It is often very hard to pull ourselves up out of the psychological and emotional quagmires that difficult bosses can create for us at work. Focusing on what we can learn from them, their difficult behaviors, their inadequacies, their approach to the world, is one way we can teach ourselves.

> I have had some VERY difficult teachers over the years (bosses, professors, relatives, strangers, etc.). Though I often resisted, I have managed to learn a great deal from them.
>
> One thing I have learned is "How not to be." From my difficult bosses, I have tried very hard not to be difficult, the way they were to me, to my own employees.

Seize ownership of the opportunity. Just because your boss doesn't appear to be interested in learning about you, doesn't mean that you can't take the opportunity to learn more about him and yourself in the bargain.

It is an indisputable truth that from every difficult situation you are in you can learn at least one important thing: either 'how to' or 'how not to'.

We may not always like the lessons the world throws in our path, but I have never seen one I couldn't learn something from. It is always worth thinking about what we can learn from any difficult situation we encounter.

Chapter 11

TAKING CARE OF YOURSELF

Difficult bosses, because of their position and authority, can make our lives miserable...if we let them. This book is about 'not letting them.' We do have that power. A big part of your success will be making sure you are taking care of the most important person in this equation – YOU.

"Be your own best Friend." (Meier)

Treat yourself as you would treat the best people in your life

When you are down – treat yourself to something that will help you get back up:

A favorite food

A meal at a favorite restaurant

A quiet evening snuggled up at home with a good movie

A decadent treat during the day (Godiva Chocolate? Or peanut M&Ms?)

A two-minute break to close your eyes and refresh

A ten-minute walk to relax (No calls!)

A nice nap

A brief meditation on positive images/thoughts

A call/meeting with an good friend (but not to gripe!)

Dream a little – you know what makes you feel good

Treat yourself well every day - you deserve it

Don't put yourself down

DO put yourself UP!

Congratulate/treat yourself when you accomplish something

Acknowledge and appreciate yourself (even if your old fogey of a boss won't...<u>especially</u> if he/she won't).

Find ways throughout your day, especially difficult days, to renew — see list above for hints, OR make up your own list and post it in your office. Just remember to look through it once in a while to remind yourself you should be taking care of YOU!

> OR...list them in some type of order, i.e. with the most decadent at the bottom of the list. Go down the list or reward yourself based on how well you feel you are doing or 'just because.' This will help you to be mindful of your choices, and the better you feel you have done, the bigger the reward! Have fun with the process. (B. Whiteway)

Appreciate, Acknowledge, and Recognize others

Our coworkers are in there slugging away, too. As a matter of fact, they probably have to put up with the same difficult behaviors that you do from your boss. If you make an effort to appreciate and recognize them, you will be doing something great for yourself in the process, AND it is highly likely that your good will and gestures will be returned many-fold over the years.

A positive work environment (see Chapter 14, "Office Dynamics") enriched by your efforts, can make a major difference over time. You have to stick to your own positivity and give it a chance to work. Even your boss will likely be affected eventually.

Taking care of your Boss IS taking care of YOU

It may be very difficult envisioning being nice to your boss, but it can pay major dividends over time.

Words of caution:

There is a fine line between being positive, kind, and nice to your boss, and going overboard into being smarmy, obsequious, or coming across as a bootlicker to your colleagues. Positivity, kindness, and appreciation are the best practices.

Hint: a great and very smart way to avoid this is to practice positivity, kindness, and appreciation with everyone at work. You treat everyone equally and the positive results multiply!

Be cautious, flexible, and take things slowly with a really difficult boss. They may be suspicious, dubious, and downright mean about kindnesses to start with, but I have seen even VERY difficult people come around, given enough time and enough of a chance to see that you are sincere.

Being Positive (appreciating, acknowledging, recognizing) your boss means:

Not letting negativity get you down or get to you in any way

Being a positive influence throughout your workplace despite others' attitudes

Doing your job and doing it well, as well as being there for your boss and others in times of need.

Being kind at appropriate moments even when they are not:

Always end conversations on a positive note

Find ways to compliment them

Always say 'thank you'

Not reacting to negativity, and finding ways to turn negativity around

Doing little things for your boss (and coworkers) when it will help make a difference

Take on some extra work

Take responsibility

Bring everyone a treat

Lighten up a meeting or gathering with some positivity/appreciation of your boss and/or others

[See also, Chapter 13, "Little Things you can do to make a BIG Difference," for more ideas.]

Self-awareness and Awareness of Others

You can make the biggest difference in your life by staying on top of how you are feeling and by understanding what actions those feelings lead to and how they are impacting others. You can then do something about the situation when it is not the way it should be.

We can have much more control over our lives than we often think.

Being careful

There are some very difficult bosses out there in the workplace, and there are even a few who are seriously psychologically ill. If you feel you are in a situation that is impossible to deal with, **please get help**. Many of the suggestions, skills, and tools in this book may help, but it is always best to err on the side of caution. Trained counselors, personal coaches, and other professionals can be helpful to you in providing an additional, knowledgeable perspective.

Serious concerns need to be taken seriously. Never put yourself or your colleagues in a dangerous position. If need be, please take your concerns to Human Resources and/or other appropriate agencies within your organizational structure.

Questions and Ideas for Contemplation

Bosses can make us feel small, bad, 'not good enough,' guilty, etc.

Actually, they can't 'make' us, but they can do a pretty good job of trying to get us to buy into their negativity. We don't have to. **Our self-worth should come from within ourselves, not from the opinions of others, good or bad.**

Come back to this Key Idea whenever you are feeling down. Brainstorm ideas to get yourself back on your feet. As you work on this you will find that less negativity will directly impact you; you will also find that you will begin to turn things around much more quickly when your self-worth does take some hits.

Take care of YOU! You deserve to be treated kindly. You are the first person in line who can do that. [Initially you may feel like the only person who is in the positivity queue.]

Stick with your positive approach and the dynamics of your office space WILL change.

Author's Note

I have written a great deal about "Taking Care of YOU" in all of my works. If you are interested in a prescription for a great life, my book, *A Perfect Day: Guide for A Better Life******* is full of great ideas to help you approach everything positively, from daily tasks to difficult concerns, as well as ideas for 'having more fun with your life and work.'

**Winner *Best Book* Non-fiction at Oklahoma Writers Federation and *Merit Award* from *Writer's Digest*. Available on-line at Amazon.com.

Chapter 12

KNOW THE BEHAVIOR

What is your attitude? Are you a helpless victim or are you

"an active participant in the co-creation of your life?"

(Betty Perkins)

People can be difficult, exasperating, uncouth, loud, rude, and, well...jerks. But when you sit down and think carefully about what it is that bothers you, it all boils down to their behavior(s).

This is a very key point:

Know the behavior

When you know exactly what bothers you, it is easier to succeed with someone, far easier than by generically thinking of them as 'difficult.' In a sense this is like breaking something down into component parts, so that each part is understandable and manageable. We can deal with a behavior; it is tougher dealing with 'a jerk.'

A very good exercise is to make an effort to delineate specifically what bothers you about your boss' behavior, attitude, demeanor, etc. Break it the types of behaviors that bother you, e.g. are they rude, belligerent, over-powering, etc. When you are done you will have a good handle on what you have to 'combat.' [See end of Chapter 18 for a specific exercise devised just for this purpose.]

Everyone is Different

The truth is we all manifest qualities and attributes in our own individual ways. You and I would likely describe the same 'difficult' boss, quite differently. Understanding what affects you about a difficult person will help you learn to deal with their behaviors more effectively.

Be Proactive about Everything

Take the bull by the horns – not your boss – but everything to do with your work life.

Ask yourself, "What can I do to make a difference? What can I do to be better/more effective?"

In my work?

In this relationship with my boss/coworkers?

In my demeanor and attitude?

By erasing negativity, and bringing positivity to my work life?

Ask yourself, "What can I do to solve this problem?" (Cava) How can I make a difference with...

The presenting behavior my boss manifests

My concerns and worries

My boss' concerns and worries (even if it is NOT your fault or responsibility)

Be a problem solver...

...rather than an accuser (Bramson). Bosses tend to like employees who are willing to step up to the plate, take responsibility for getting things done, making things right, and even owning up to mistakes.

You do not necessarily have to accept blame; but you CAN charge into the fray and offer to make an effort to "get it right" and "get it done." [Two key 'intents' of difficult bosses. See Chapter 9, "Knowing Your Boss"]

Personal Power

"When you take responsibility for problems or concerns that come across your desk, you have created the possibility of finding a solution. Taking responsibility is personal empowerment!"

(Speech to American Business Women's Association, 2007)

Help your boss to save face. By taking responsibility and being proactive about digging in and finding solutions to problems you empower yourself and your relationship with your boss.

Stay focused on **what needs to be done, not who is to blame**. Most bosses will remember who went to bat for them. Don't wait until evaluation time. Making an effort on your boss' behalf can help turn an ogre into a lamb and often, very quickly. (Bramson)

"His ease is your ease." (Hoover)

Many bosses are difficult because they see the world around them as being difficult. Whatever you can do to help assuage that perspective is a very effective means of changing office dynamics. It may also help to change your boss' approach to nearly everyone and everything. (See the next Chapter for many ideas related to this important concept.) It is important to jump on this bandwagon early. We all feel better, and thus typically interact with others and the world better, when other people support and encourage us.

Remember:

"Difficult people become even more difficult when they are misunderstood." (Bell and Smith)

OR,

very importantly,

perceive to be misunderstood. (Koob)

"How comfortable does your boss feel around you?" (Hoover)

If it is as uncomfortable as you feel around him/her, you need to adjust. It is not likely he/she is going to adjust to you! Find ways to ease his fears — keep in mind that difficult behavior is rooted in insecurity and personal fear.

Don'ts

I'm a 'Do' sort of person and tend not to focus on negatives, but here is a short list of things NOT to do with your boss:

> Don't yell, argue, fight back, challenge their authority — the odds are nearly 100% you will lose. Even if you don't lose immediately, you will certainly lose in the long run.

> Don't rebel or foment rebellion — ditto above; there are much better ways to change things. Be proactive.

Don't try to show your boss the error of his ways or to prove him wrong, point out mistakes, or criticize – directly or to others. Remember, things always get around in an office. Avoid one-upmanship (Lubit) – another losing proposition in both the short and long runs.

Don't ever humiliate your boss or try to put him in an uncomfortable position with others. Stay on top of what you say and how you say it. Watch for their reaction to what you say and do.

Don't ever go behind your boss' back, unless you specifically let them know you need to talk to someone higher up. Hopefully, you can get your boss' approval to do this.

OR if you are truly in an impossible situation with your boss and you are seeking proactive ways to deal with it, you can go to Human Resources or your boss' supervisor for assistance and advice on what to do next. If you do choose to go to another authority figure, always go with the attitude that "I am seeking a positive solution to this concern," and "I am willing to make every effort to work for a solution myself, but I feel I need some assistance."

Remember that 'POWER' thing

Bosses have the power to affect our lives in many ways. Small victories achieved through negativity will often turn into major losses down the road. Bosses have long memories. If you have started out on the wrong foot, you will have some work to do, very positive-oriented work, to get back on the plus side.

Yes, you can whine, complain, blame, go to HR, go behind your boss' back to his boss, etc. But unless you have tried everything else or the situation really IS impossible, your best chance, if you plan to remain in this job, is to work with him/her in a positive, proactive way.

Get and Keep your boss involved

Bosses will be less difficult and more proactively involved with you if you **help them to be involved**. There are always ways to elicit their input, acceptance, knowledge, resources, etc., in positive ways. The more they feel a part of what you are doing, and can take part in reaping the benefits of your fine work, the better your working relationship will likely be.

Keep your boss informed

As long as you can be brief and to the point, I cannot imagine too many bosses who will not appreciate your keeping them in on what you are doing and accomplishing for the team.

Information flow upward, if done right, is a very positive way to help keep difficult bosses from being difficult. [See Chapters 15-17 on Communications and Information]

Be the BEST you can be

Though there are a few boss types who won't necessarily appreciate your high-quality work and your success, most will. Even the few who don't, may get more on your bandwagon the more you can make them part of what you are doing and accomplishing.

When you can couch your success in terms of their success, and in terms of the team's success as seen through the eyes of their boss, they are more likely to come on board and help you.

Circumstances dictate the Response (Weiss)

We can give you the best knowledge, skills, and tools we know for you to be successful with your difficult boss; however, we can't be in your shoes when you need to interact with them. Learn, practice, and plan. Then stay flexible and alert to adjust as situations dictate. It is very common for difficult people to find new ways to irritate you, if what they are doing stops having an effect. Part of their need for power and control may be to illicit certain kinds of responses from you.

Adjust as you need to, but stick to your positive track through your self-worth and self-control. Eventually, they will get the point – that you no longer intend to play their games.

Questions and Ideas for Contemplation

There is a ton of good advice in this chapter. As you read the rest of this book, come back here to get re-rooted in some of the Key Ideas that can drive your success.

Also, keep in mind that the entire first part of this book deals with the basics of being successful with difficult people/bosses. Especially review "The Seven Keys to Being Successful with Difficult People"

Self-awareness

Self-worth

Self-confidence

Self-control

Honesty

Kindness

Positivity

Chapter 13

THINGS YOU CAN DO TO MAKE A BIG DIFFERENCE

"Deliberately scheme how you can be a positive influence in your work place." (John Hoover)

Positive attention

The more positive attention we pay to our boss, the less likely he/she will use negatively presenting behaviors with us. We all like to be noticed. We especially like to be recognized and appreciated. We can do this in many different ways without being obsequious or overdoing it. Regardless of whether or not your boss is an ogre, create a pleasant aura from the get-go.

Here are some great ideas

Make personal, friendly contact every day – the earlier in the day the better

A pleasant hello

A very brief good morning, hope you have a great day e-mail (sent from home or before he gets in – let him know you are up, active, and involved). You may not want to do this every day, but once or twice a week is great.

A pleasant personal remark before or after a meeting

A question that reflects your interest in him or his family's well-being

A thank you or compliment at an appropriate moment

Be positive around the office and with team members

His/her administrative assistant is a KEY person to be kind to. When you are nice, complimentary, etc. to them, your boss will hear about it, even if indirectly.

Any positivity you add during the day with your team members gets around. You can be the positive force that starts to turn your office dynamics in the right direction. [See next Chapter]

Be interested in your boss and your team members. Interest is a form of acknowledgement – something most of us can use a lot more of.

Give genuine compliments for a week. (Littauer) Give them to your team members AND your boss – spread the good vibes around. Then make an effort to keep it up ad infinitum.

You have to pay attention to people and the good things they are doing for this to be effective. Paying positive attention to someone is a good thing in and of itself. It is a form of acknowledgement. Everyone likes to be appreciated.

Reward positivity in your boss

Here is a good piece of advice relevant to behavior modification techniques which can work well with most difficult bosses, and sometimes even the really difficult bosses. As always, be judicious:

Be upbeat, attentive, appreciative, smiling, and eager to please whenever your boss behaves/acts in ways you like. Be neutral, silent, and non-reactive when he/she behaves in ways that displease you.

I never advocate negativity, but neutrality can work just as well, as long as it is markedly different from the positive you. Keep in mind that tactics like ignoring your boss may seem like a neutral approach, but may be perceived as being negative. Use your best judgment in choosing what will work in different situations.

Key Point: **Perceptions are everything.** It is always about how someone takes something; not about what you meant. Adjust if what you are doing is not being seen in the positive light you are aiming for.

Find ways to turn their negativity around through your own positivity. For example, when they seem grumpy or out-of-sorts, find a way to help cheer them up – use some humor, a kind act, etc. Then when you see a positive change as a result, acknowledge and reward THAT behavior.

Thank them for feedback – negative or positive.

'Thanking' is almost always a positive approach and it shows you have paid attention, are willing to accept responsibility, and to make an effort to always do your best.

Do things that warrant positive attention to yourself (Hoover)

Find ways to help your boss/team members out

Be willing to take on responsibility and risks (Bramson)

Be willing to share kudos (especially with your boss). An email:

> "I'm really glad the contract I wrote got accepted by B & J Industries. I couldn't have done it without your support and encouragement, Darla."

Keep your boss apprised of the positive things you are doing for him/her, your team, the organization Keep it brief and to the point.

Support your boss and team members through difficulties and concerns.

Ask: "What can I do to help?" "Is there anything you want me to do to help get this done, to make this right?"

Strive at making your work, your team, your boss, and the organization the best it can be. Let your boss know that this is what you are striving to accomplish.

Be flexible and accommodating (Lubit)

Flexibility, creativity, out-of-the-box thinking, **when coupled with keeping your boss apprised and a part of what you are doing,** can be very effective in alleviating concerns, especially if your boss tends to block new ideas and discourages change.

Accommodate their pet areas and projects whenever possible, too. They will appreciate your support.

Acknowledge and recognize your boss' strengths and competencies (Bramson)

We all like to hear good things about ourselves on occasion. Be sure not to overdo this. Obsequiousness is not becoming from either side of the coin.

Do the unexpected (Brinkman and Kirschner)

Be willing to take a chance. It is more fun; keeps you alive and active; and if judiciously planned can yield unexpectedly positive results. Be cautious and smart when using this technique, but a pleasant surprise can be very powerful.

Go the extra mile

Set up a team/boss recognition day

Suggest or throw a get-together to reward everyone for a job well done

Use your imagination, but always consider your boss' personality and what you think he/she may appreciate.

> I have done some wild and crazy things in my day to/with people in authority positions over me, but I had a good feel for how these ideas would be taken. They always yielded positive results.

Be Yourself

Bring the core values and qualities you hold close to your heart into work with you. Don't let your boss' or others' negativity throw you off track. When we can stay in touch with the truth of who we are, we can have a dramatic affect on all those around us.

Questions and Ideas for Contemplation

Take the various sub-headings in this section and brainstorm specific ideas you could implement to make a difference right away at work. Keep at it and come back to it several times during the week. You might be surprised after a week's jottings, how many good ideas you have. Try some of them out. Keep your list handy (in your desk), so as you go through your work week you can remind yourself of the positive influence you can have.

Chapter 14

OFFICE DYNAMICS

The relationships and space in which we do business are critical to our success at work. Bosses tend to have a major influence on the dynamics in and around the office. However, keep in mind that every member of a team/division has the potential to add a great deal to the overall tenor of those workplace dynamics. Paying attention to how specific relationships influence your workplace is very important to your ability to make the most of your work life.

Every workspace and culture is different. However, they all have something in common – everything works off of everything else. There is a system, for better or for worse, that in different ways drives the relationships of the people in it.

A work system is like a family system. **How one person interacts in and impacts the system affects all the relationships close to that person in the system.**

In a family, the parents and children all interact to uphold the status quo of the family system, good or bad. Grandparents and other relatives also have an impact on the family. The culture of the family system has a long history, and much of the dynamics within a family group have come down through both sides of the family over many years. There is a balance, whether it works well or not, that has become an accepted way of doing things in the family. When someone tries to change that, the rest of the system reacts to re-balance itself.

Work is the same in many ways. Regardless of level, position, or job description the entire staff affects the way the system works. When something or someone is not working well in the system, it impacts everyone. And here is the really important point – **everyone** has, in some way, an impact on what continues in the system, good or bad.

Keep your eyes and ears open

Know what elements seem to dictate the overall atmosphere you work in. Pay particular attention to key individuals, including your boss, and how they seem to affect (or infect!) the team.

It is very common for one or two individuals to dominate or seem to dominate an office's general atmosphere. Negativity in almost any form – from anyone, especially authority figures – can affect everyone's ability to function at a high level and will often infect individuals' and the team's general attitude and demeanor.

The infectious nature of negativity

Choose any type of difficult boss (See Chapter 19), and you can easily envision how their approach to others, their difficult behaviors, can dramatically affect an entire group.

Add to this mix one or more other team members who buy into the boss' negativity, or choose to wallow in their own negative reactions to the boss' negativity, and you have an extremely unpleasant office situation in which to work. "Negativity breeds Negativity."

The infectious nature of positivity

Being consistently positive can have an even greater affect over time, IF one or more team members stick to their guns. It takes at least one person on the team to make an extraordinary effort to infuse positivity at every opportunity. [See Chapter 13 for lots of good ideas, and take some time to brainstorm many more for yourself and your team members.]

Positivity breeds Positivity

It actually does, and though in a really depressed atmosphere it may not seem like it, there is a good chance of turning things around, given perseverance by one or more people. Most people would much rather follow others who are positive and upbeat than to accept/wallow in negativity. Compliments, appreciation, acknowledgement, recognition, thanks, used judiciously and regularly can change frowns to smiles, and help turn 'down' days to 'up' days, and depression and lethargy to enthusiasm and energy. IT IS POSSIBLE!

What it takes

It takes being kind to everyone.

It takes being open and honest.

It takes a positive approach that rejects criticism, defensiveness, complaining, blaming, and whining.

It takes being compassionate, especially to those who are suffering from their own negativity.

It takes your willingness to support others, even if they are negative (to start with).

It takes personal strength and perseverance.

It takes positive talk, positive thought, and sharing positive feelings.

People will notice. You may not change the curmudgeons in the group, but chances are everyone will be 'infected' over time.

You don't have to be a particularly bubbly, out-going person. Just make a decision to add positivity instead of negativity.

Working in Limited Space

Everything said, done, felt, and thought about has ramifications in the limited space of an office. You may think things are confidential, but chances are someone will find out or possibly insinuate things from the many cues that we give off emotionally.

Being honest and open about who you are and what you do is the best way to deal with subterfuge in others, regardless of whether or not the atmosphere in your office is typically clandestine/ secretive. While some people may never learn to be open and forthright, your example can make a difference for many team members.

You do have to be careful about what you say and how you say it. You should not discuss close personal issues at work unless you really feel comfortable doing so and sincerely trust the person you are with. Even then it is wise to be judicious. However, I am a firm believer that office and work issues are best out-in-the-open. When we or others hide things at work, the place can quickly become a nest of intrigue centered around information, the lack of information, and misinformation.

Though you may have to deal with someone claiming your work or efforts, the likelihood is small if you are communicating openly and honestly, because you will be keeping people apprised of what you are about on a regular basis. [See Chapters 15 -17 on Communication and Information]

P.S.

Always keep notes, e-mails, memos, and other documentation of key communications and of your work.

You can help set the stage

I have seen negative team members and bosses have a devastating effect on an entire team's morale. I have also seen the opposite – a positive influence – make huge changes to a team, and even to an entire organization. If you are not happy with the dynamics of the place you work in, then work to make a difference. It IS possible, but it does take courage, fortitude, positive determination, and above all, kindness and compassion for others.

Questions and Ideas for Contemplation

Staying out of the loop of office politics, gossip, and intrigue is not always easy. Our best defense is the 'offense of positivity.' Create the atmosphere you would like to work in by being an example.

I have a motto I think of often, "If you are not having fun, something's wrong – adjust." I truly believe life and work are to be enjoyed. It is up to me to fulfill this idea/ideal; I make myself responsible for my own fun. You can too. Start making a difference today.

Chapter 15

COMMUNICATIONS

The Right Stuff at the Right Time

Positive, open, and direct communications are essential to succeeding with a difficult boss. YOU have to be the catalyst for this, because generally, if you have concerns with an authority figure, part of those concerns will have to do with the way they communicate with you. Your ability to communicate well, as well as the style in which you communicate with a person above you in the chain of command, can make or break your relationship.

> I have written a great deal about good fundamental communications with difficult people at work. For a solid basis in essential techniques, see representative chapters in *Understanding and Working with Difficult People*; *Dealing with Difficult Customers*; and *Succeeding with Difficult Coworkers*. This Chapter and the next two will focus specifically on Communications with Authority/ Power figures.

Negativity NEVER helps

You can be as 'right' as you want to be about the other person, i.e. their lack of skills, their lying, their complaining and blaming, their negativity, but in almost every instance POWER will be the overriding factor in who 'wins' in the long run.

Make a decision right now that **being right** is hardly ever worth all the fuss it engenders. **It is far better to be kind.** It is possible to learn the proper techniques and skills to communicate effectively so that 'being right' rarely enters the picture, especially in the long run.

Lose a few battles if you have to; win the war.

Never compete with your boss

This isn't really a war and those aren't battles you fight with him/her every day. They may feel like it because you ARE fighting back and/or feel like you are losing, but they don't ever have to be. Find ways to work with and support your boss, and to facilitate what she wants to get accomplished. You are much more likely to gain her respect, support, and good will over time if you do.

Help your boss be positive

Whether your boss rants and raves, is rude and uncouth, or hardly says anything at all, his Communication skills are based on:

Learning – experience, observation, etc.

Getting his intent fulfilled (e.g. 'Get it Done,' 'Get it Right,' etc., see Chapter 9 for discussion on 'Intent')

What has worked in the past for him, and what seems to work now, i.e. what has filled his needs, wants, and desires no matter however disruptive that may have been or is.

Personal negative feelings of inferiority, guilt, fear, etc.

To effect positive change in your boss and his approach to you (and hopefully others), you have to change the dynamics behind his style. In short:

If your boss has learned to communicate in difficult ways, help to teach him new, better, more effective, kinder ways to get his point across. NOT directly, but indirectly by changing how you approach him.

Fulfill his intent; help fulfill his needs, wants, desires – before he gets upset!

Help him understand that other, better, more kind communications are more effective with you (and others).

Listen!

Listen carefully to what he says – especially criticism. We can learn a great deal from our boss even if we don't feel it is all deserved.

A common frustration of bosses is that some employees can't or won't accept any constructive criticism. Employees who are defensive, who consistently blame others, and who always have excuses, rarely have the respect of their bosses. Even if the behavior is surreptitious, or behind-their-back, the boss will know.

Develop an understanding of your boss (and yourself) through these interactions. Show that you are willing to work at improving areas of concern. This does work, and it feels so much better than being defensive and blaming others. Remember defensiveness invariably lowers their perception of who we are. You can always say something akin to, "I'm not sure I completely agree with this assessment, but I understand what you are saying. I will keep on top of this and try to do better. I appreciate your input and advice at any time."

Listen for understanding.

Listen carefully, because it shows respect and is a form of acknowledgement.

Listen so they will also pay attention to what you have to say, when it is your turn. When you respect what they say, it is much more likely they will be willing to listen and respect what you have to say.

Listen for content.

Listen attentively because they will respect you for it.

Help Reeducate your Boss

Your style, and especially your self-control in communicating, will speak volumes. You can also reinforce your positive actions through appropriate, well-placed comments. For example,

Support what they are saying; it shows you are listening and it acknowledges them:

"That's a great point."

"I see what you are getting at. I like it!"

Reinforce their positive communications:

"That's great,"

"Thanks, I appreciate that."

Let them know what you appreciate and honor as well:

"Thanks Jennie, I appreciate quality, too. We're on the same page."

"That's great, Steve, being forthright with this will help everyone on the team."

Through careful listening and by using carefully crafted comments, you can help sculpt conversations that help not only improve your relationship with your boss, but also set the stage for more controlled and better communications in the future.

If you have an explosive, aggressive boss, staying calm and in-control will typically change their approach to you. They are expecting you to fight back and defend yourself, or to cringe, apologize, and/or feel guilty. When you don't react to their behavior in a way they expect, they will notice. If you stay controlled and centered, and are able to respond to their outbursts calmly, you will be at least half-way there.

Useful techniques:

Stand or sit upright

>   Maintain an unchallenging eye contact

>   Respond in a clear, controlled voice (don't try to match their volume)

>   Sound concerned and helpful

>   If they are really irate, repeat their name over and over until they calm enough for you to say something else.

>   Let them wind down before offering anything specific to the concern they have raised.

You CAN, and in many cases should, say things like:

>   "John, I can see you are upset about something. I am ready to deal with this, please calm down and I will make every effort to understand what has happened and get right on a solution."

Here you tell them, very kindly, but honestly, that their communication style is not something you appreciate. At the same time, you offer understanding, and a proactive, solution-driven approach.

Or, this:

"You are right, Anne, there is a problem here. Let me get right on it and I will find a way to get this done right."

Be willing to admit if you are wrong or made a mistake. Be willing to accept responsibility to make things better, even if it is not your fault or your responsibility. Help is almost always appreciated and so will be your proactive approach, your willingness to jump into the fray.

DON'T offer excuses, even if it is not your fault or not part of your responsibilities. Bosses see excuses as weakness. Don't use the word 'but.' It qualifies everything that went before.

"...but you should know that this is Steve's area."

This statement points a finger, makes an excuse, insinuates your boss doesn't know whose area it is (which is insulting), and qualifies your offer of help.

"...but I didn't create this mess."

This is also an excuse and you are pointing a broad finger away from you. Your boss will respond to positive, goal-directed behavior. Anything less diminishes you in her eyes.

Use behavior-modification techniques

"Rewarded behavior is repeated behavior" –

even if the behavior is accidental. (Hoover)

Praise positive, open, direct, honest communications from your boss; be neutral, assertive, in-control when he uses a poor approach. Again, always remember to never show any negativity.

An Example

Your boss comes in and tells you, in fairly neutral terms, but with a somewhat negative tone, that you got something wrong on a big report. How do you respond? Can you choose a constructive approach that sets the stage for improving your communications with him?

"Bob, I appreciate your letting me know about this concern right away. I will deal with it immediately and work to make sure I'm on top of this type of issue in the future. Your openness about this will help me improve my efforts. I want to thank you for bringing this to my attention."

Here you respond positively. Even though there was some negativity to his method, at least he didn't explode like he usually does. Always use their name – it makes it more personal and enhances the positive. You reinforce his 'better' behavior by not being defensive, and you even reinforce behavior you would like to see, though it wasn't actually there, by staying positive despite the negative overtones to his approach. These types of nuances to communications can be very powerful and leading.

Understand what they are after

Use neutral and positive communications to find out what the concern is and what the bottom line is. When someone is understood, and, more importantly, perceives that the other person is making an effort to understand what they want, their communications will almost always improve. Do this a number of times and your boss will see that you want to understand what they want. The general dynamics of your interactions should improve.

Revisiting intent

'Get it done' bosses

Focus in on what they want to get done – do this right away and offer to 'get right on it.' In general, be a 'get it done' kind of person even if you are more of a 'get it right' person. Develop a "Can Do' attitude. (Brinkman and Kirschner; Hoover)

'Get it right' bosses

This type of boss can be incredibly picky and critical. Pay close attention to what 'right' means to them, and try to let them know you will make every effort to provide it. Keep a notebook handy and take notes on what they say. They will very likely see this as a positive characteristic, i.e. you are concerned with 'getting it right,' too.

'Need to get along' bosses

There is a fine line between being a buddy to an authority figure and maintaining professional distance and decorum. Help 'need to get along' bosses be a part of what is happening in the office. Your communications with them start with friendliness and regular contact: make it a point to say 'hi' every day; send them an upbeat, friendly (brief!) morning e-mail; keep them apprised and 'into' what is happening, etc.

'Need to be appreciated' bosses

We all want and need to feel appreciated (and recognized). Some of us need this more than others. ALL bosses will respond to your showing appreciation for who they are, what they do, and the concerns they have. Use your best judgment and trial and error to figure how much of this they need on a regular basis:

'Thank you,'

'Great presentation,'

'I like that suggestion you made.'

And so on

Remember: Positivity breeds Positivity.

'Need to be cared for' bosses

I truly believe that showing some sincere caring for people throughout the workplace, including that ogre who is your boss, will erase many difficulties. 'Caring' means the recognition that we are all human, we are all in this together, and we can all help everyone else do a better job:

"Joyce, I feel really bad that we didn't get the Johnson contract. I know you had your heart set on that one. Is there any way I can help with what is on your plate now?"

"Andy, just wanted to let you know I am here for you, if you need any help while you are under the weather. Hope you feel better."

Human contact is best; but memos and e-mails, birthday cards, kind words over the phone, all can make a big difference.

Worried about appearing obsequious? Appreciate, acknowledge, recognize, care for everyone on your team and it will become 'just who you are.' You won't be seen as singling out your boss for special treatment.

It has worked in the past

We all tend to use behaviors that have gotten us what we wanted, needed, thought we needed, desired. Difficult bosses probably are using the same techniques they have always used because no one has ever challenged them. You CAN and SHOULD challenge them... but do so kindly.

> "Bill, I am here for you, but I am having a little difficulty understanding what you really want. Can we sit down and work through this? I will take responsibility for the outcome, so don't worry. If I get off-track, just set me straight. You know this stuff better than I do..."

An uncommunicative boss can be especially trying. You have a deadline, something has been dropped in your lap with minimal input, and you are feeling lost because your boss cannot seem to communicate what he wants you to do. His comfort zone is saying as little as possible and hoping you will go do something without him having to take any responsibility.

Uncommunicative bosses are protecting themselves. To communicate with them effectively you have to find ways for them to feel safe. It does take time and patience, and any negativity will send them deeper into their shell. When they do open up, reinforce it:

> "Wow, that's a great idea. I'm going to work that in. This will look much better when we send it up the line."

How they FEEL

Your boss' communications are a window into his/her personality. The way they interact, respond, tell, direct, critique, etc. all say a tremendous amount about who they are and what is driving them. Understanding that difficult behaviors are predicated by very difficult to deal with emotions is paramount to your success.

People who regularly exhibit difficult behaviors are dealing with inferiority and poor self-image issues. You may be able to commiserate because their difficult behavior is raising some of the same issues in you. If you are feeling 'less than' or 'not-good-enough,' what helps make you feel better?

Answer this question and then apply it to your boss!

What will make my boss feel better?

Here are some hints:

Being appreciated

Being respected

Being acknowledged for who we are and what we do

Being recognized

Feeling understood

Basic human contact and kindnesses

Being supported

There are always ways to support and recognize even VERY difficult people. Do so, and they will change. It is virtually guaranteed, IF you stay away from negativity.

Questions and Ideas for Contemplation

You will see many more examples related to these ideas throughout the rest of this text. Other basic techniques and skills will also be discussed as we detail being successful with various 'difficult boss types.'

One of the hardest elements in communications with a difficult boss to get beyond is 'how they approach us.' Their negativity can, and often does, affect us very strongly. That is why knowing yourself, and coupling that self-knowledge with the understandings discussed in this book, make a powerful set of tools for you to use in being successful with a difficult authority figure.

Chapter 16

OVER-COMMUNICATING

"Am I really present for (listening to) this person,

or am I trying to change them?" (Betty Perkins)

"Telling a person why you are telling them something before you actually tell them is a simple method for directing attention where you want it to go." (Brinkman and Kirshner)

It is very rare indeed that there is too much communicating going on in a business. Usually the opposite is true, and unfortunately it seems to get worse the higher one gets in an organization. Here is a very key point: **it is very unlikely that you are communicating enough with the key people in your organization, most notably your boss.**

Kick it into High Gear

Bosses, like all of us, like to be in the know. With some types of bosses, notably nitpickers, highly-critical types, and micro-managers, you can hardly do too much communicating.

BUT! There are some keys to over-communicating well

Over-communicating: Key Ideas

Keep it brief

Bosses like information, not fluff (see next chapter). If you are taking up their time with mundane details or your extra-curricular activities, that is not communicating effectively or professionally. [This doesn't mean you shouldn't include an occasional appreciative, acknowledging comment. These are positive inclusions, but keep them brief.]

Keep on track

It is better to detail one specific issue and meet several times, than to go meandering about. This is especially true of memos and e-mails. A good rule of thumb is one issue per e-mail. Send another brief e-mail if you want to cover some more ground.

Be on time

Or better yet, be ahead of time. Great for 'get-it-done' bosses, and it also shows well when evaluation time comes around. Far too many individuals and businesses operate on a last-minute-basis.

Keep them apprised of anything important

I can read an e-mail that says, "Ed, the Hauser contract was at FedEx at 7:22 this morning. Just thought you would like an update. Have a great day, Joe," in a few seconds, delete it, and move on. But believe me, I will remember and it will make a difference to my day, because I won't have to worry about whether you are on top of things. [I am also more likely to see you in a different light the more you do these kinds of things.]

Ask

If they need more information

What kind of information they want from you on a regular basis

What information they need relative to a specific issue or project

How and by what means they prefer you to communicate with them

And so on.

Asking is a great communication tool that we don't use nearly enough. It often shows respect for another person's ideas and it can open many closed doors. Remember to ask kindly.

Asking questions IS positive communication

Asking helps keep YOU on top of things, and there is no reason to be timid about it. Be assertive and positive about information flow. Asking helps show concern, indicates your interest in assisting, and shows you have personal strength.

Paraphrase

Paraphrasing is a technique we also don't use enough.

Too often communicating concerns are not a result of effort, but of misunderstanding or incomplete information. When in doubt, ask. When involved in a conversation, ALWAYS do some paraphrasing. It is a good habit to get into.

Paraphrasing aids communication flow in many ways:

It denotes understanding AND non-understanding on the part of the person who is paraphrasing. It helps you get it right.

It shows you are listening and interested in what the other person is saying.

It helps you clarify intent, details, understandings.

It opens the door for further understanding.

It creates a type of respect and control in a conversation.

It helps with memory. Repetition is the mother of memory, and rephrasing something in your own words is the best way to do that.

It helps provide feedback to the speaker about how well they are communicating, and it does it in a far less damaging way than either one or both people being upset later because someone didn't get it right.

Provide feedback

Giving feedback to your boss is something you CAN and should do. It can be done effectively and positively without ruffling his/her feathers.

"Betty, I didn't quite understand what you had in mind for the Geyer contract. Could we take two minutes to clarify this?"

"Whoa there, Harry! That went over my head. Sorry. Could we back up and go through that again. I think I need to ask a couple of questions."

"Roberta, we sincerely appreciate your taking the time to go over this new procedure with us. I'm not sure about everyone else in the room, but I'm a bit lost. Would you be willing to take a few questions at this point?"

Specificity can work wonders

When in doubt, ask, and be willing to ask again and again, more and more specifically, until you get to where you need to be. Most bosses will not be upset IF you:

Are focused and interested

Couch things in terms of getting it done or getting it right (or both). Be willing to SAY IT:

"Tom, I want to make sure we get this right so there aren't any mistakes when we send it up the chain of command. Could you tell us..."

Let them know you have their, the team's, and/or the organization's best interests in mind. Again, SAY IT. Don't expect them to assume this.

"Sandra, if you give us a bit more specific information on how you want us to proceed, we should be able to make this look really good for Laura (Sandra's boss)."

Negativity Revisited

Accuse your boss – expect a counterattack

Complain – they'll know it, and it is a sign of weakness. (Bramson)

Blame – is also a sign of weakness, even if someone else IS at fault.

Whine – Is this the real YOU? The YOU that you want to show the world? Is it the YOU that you want to show your boss and coworkers?

Positivity works so much better

Get things out in the open

I am a firm believer in getting things out in the open so they are NOT discussed behind people's backs. This is the only true defense one has against liars and back-stabbers. Be willing to ask and discuss whatever is important, while remaining neutral and non-accusatory. Be willing to talk about your concerns.

Sneaky people have a hard time being sneaky when someone is willing to talk about anything and everything openly. This also goes for bosses.

Written memo to a boss who commonly steals everyone's work and takes credit by himself; copies sent to all team members:

> "Max, good news! We are having a celebration of the acceptance of the Bingood contract after work today in the lounge. You are on the spot to give a short speech to the team about the good work they did, because with your leadership we were able to get this done. I have taken the liberty to invite Sandra and the other Senior Directors in the matrix. They will want to congratulate you, too. We plan a few awards for key people and I know you'll want to congratulate them as well.
>
> Best, Steve.
>
> P.S. The team appreciates all your support on this one!

There are ALWAYS positive ways to say things!

Another positive result is that this keeps everyone who worked on the project in the loop for reaping benefits from its success.

When you get YOUR Chance

Communicating your ideas positively and assertively is also a critical area to consider. Most importantly always try to couch things in terms of taking responsibility for what you say:

> Tell them it is YOUR truth, not THE truth. (Brinkman and Kirschner)
>
> Good listening and understanding should precede positive communications on your end. People are much more likely to listen to you, if you have listened well to them.
>
> Be direct and reasonable – it is respectful. (Rosen)
>
> Use, "I," it denotes ownership and accepting responsibility for what you say. "I feel...," I think..." "I would like to..."
>
> > "You," tends to be accusatory and demanding. "You did..." "You didn't..." Or, "You should have...," "You shouldn't have..."

'We' can also be a good choice if you are not using it to avoid responsibility. It can bring your boss and coworkers into the mix as far as what you are doing, what you want to do, and/or what you have accomplished. Sharing effort and positive results can create better overall team/boss relationships and a better overall office atmosphere.

"We really got some good results with the Barber contract."

"If we pull together on this, I think we will have a great chance at a positive outcome."

Acknowledge your boss and what she says before you give your ideas (Even if what she said was conveyed negatively). It is courteous, supports her, and creates good will.

"How you communicate is as vital as what you communicate." (Osbourne)

Pay attention to your voice intonation and volume, your posture, gestures, facial expressions, word choices, phrasing, etc.

Present your views indirectly – use 'maybe,' 'perhaps;' 'might,' plural pronouns 'we,' 'us;' ask leading questions (Brinkman and Kirschner)

"I was thinking that this might be another way we could look at this problem. What do you think?"

Asking them for their input, opinion, ideas is respectful, recognizes their value, and helps make them a part of your ideas.

Help your boss be part of your ideas (even if he didn't help at all). It is smart politics and doesn't really take anything away from your work.

"Something you said last week kicked this idea off in my head, Paul. What do you think of..."

Don't give bad news unless you offer a solution with a proactive, 'I am willing to help' attitude. (Toropov)

"I know this data is not good news, Bob, however I do think we could consider making a few changes based on a couple of ideas I have generated. Would you like to take a look at this? What do you think should be our next step? I'm ready to tackle whatever direction you want to go."

Ask for their opinion and input: this helps get them on board and invested in your ideas.

"That's how I see this in a nutshell, Vickie. I really value your insight and. I know with your input we can make this design even better."

It is not as hard as it may seem

When I coach executives, I am often asked 'how do I say X'. It might be some bad news they have to give, an evaluation process that needs to be done, or just something they are uncomfortable communicating and can't seem to find the right, positive way to do so. After a few minutes of asking questions and brainstorming, we always come up with a solution. With the help of some leading questions, they can find much more positive ways to communicate with their employees, colleagues, and their own bosses. The more you try this, the easier it becomes. Coaching and practice both help.

You will see more examples throughout this book, but keep in mind that there are always better ways to say things if you take some time to think about not only what you have to say, but **how it will impact the person you are saying it to.** When it comes to bosses, that IS smart business.

Questions and Ideas for Contemplation

Take a week and make an effort to step-up your communications with your boss and your fellow team members. Try 'over-communicating' and see if you notice any changes in the way people see you. I would be very surprised if you don't receive some positive feedback fairly quickly.

Chapter 17

INFORMATION

"Your objective is to let the difficult boss know that *every one* of the memos you (regularly) send along results in a positive action or recommendation of some kind." (Toporov)

A matter of <u>Survival</u>

The flow of information between you and your boss, and your boss and your team IS that important!

There is a good chance your difficult boss doesn't get it, i.e. the absolute importance of an open flow of information up, and especially down the chain. Many employees of difficult bosses have considerable concerns about the amount and quality of the information they receive from their boss. These are very legitimate concerns. However, there is something that can be done.

Information works two ways

Open up the channels!

Your boss could be a type that...

> Generally mistrusts people

> Is paranoid about saying too much or the wrong thing

> Uses information to control or as a power move

> Is quiet and reserved in general and rarely gives out anything unless absolutely necessary (from his perspective!).

> Expects you to understand or read her mind even though she never offers enough information

> And so on

The Onus is thus on You

Your boss is not going to change – certainly not if you just wish she would. There are ways to facilitate the flow of information and to even get your boss to open up more:

Over communicate

Keep your information flowing, and never let up. This is especially key with exacting types of bosses, e.g. the overly critical, nitpickers, micro-managers, 'get-it-done' types, etc. [See below for how to keep information flowing up and down the chain.]

Get it down on paper. The more you have in writing the better.

Take notes of key ideas, responsibilities, questions you need answered, etc., at all meetings, team and individual. Notes provide you back-up, help with keeping you on track, and can be immensely helpful with feedback. Be very specific about the things that are most important.

Make sure you write things down in your own words. This is a key memory technique and helps you keep terse, to-the-point notes.

> Hint: you might think taking this many notes will be incredibly time consuming. The truth is in the vast majority of interactions between people (individually or in groups) very little of real substance is covered. The pith can be written down in a few brief sentences and short paragraphs with some listing of items for specificity.

Write lots of brief, informative memos to your boss and to your team members. This works great IF you keep them short (readable in a few seconds), to-the-point (highlight key points), and regular.

Keep copies of ANYTHING that might be of use later on. Err on the side of too much rather than too little when storing memos and e-mails. I have seen far too many managers and employees who rue having erased a critical e-mail or thrown away a memo that would later have proven to be most valuable relevant to a concern that has arisen.

> Make hard copies of the most important items.

> Create a file of important e-mails and memos

> File notes that are key to projects, etc.

Store disks with 'old' material on them – you never know what might prove useful down the road.

Copy your boss on anything and everything that might be important to you and your team. It is also wise to copy other people on really significant documents so there is a paper or e-trail.

ASK!

Some bosses are experts at dodging issues and decisions. Ask, ask, ask.

Ask in person, and consistently seek more specificity if they insist on dodging you. Be ready with your note pad when you ask questions. It will show your boss that you are serious about some answers and plan to take action.

Ask safely: in other words, make it SAFE for your boss to answer. Be willing to take responsibility, accept challenges, offer to help, etc. The more they understand your willingness to take things on your shoulders and to support them 'through thick and thin' the more likely they will begin to share more.

Show appreciation every time you do get something out of them – especially important with close-mouthed, information-tight bosses.

> "That's great, Carl. That bit of information will help this project a lot, and I'm sure Ann will notice your contribution when we send it up the line."

When in doubt about information, your responsibilities, team or other colleagues' responsibilities, etc., ASK!

"Obtain written directions whenever possible." (Hoover)

Get things in writing from your boss. That may be down-right hard to do, but it is worth asking. When you don't get any response, then you have to take the initiative – get it in writing even if you have to write it yourself...

Write it down yourself

Do you have:

> A boss that won't commit?

Won't give out information?

Won't let you know what your responsibilities are?

Respond in writing: you can insert a great deal in a short memo that specifies what responsibilities you believe you have, what actions you plan to take, what your understanding is, etc. Then you have documented whatever you need to document.

> "Gene, my understanding is that I have responsibility for maintaining the equipment in section A of building 182 and that Darla is taking on section B. My additional responsibilities are to Delta team when they need extra help. Let me know if this is not correct. Thanks."

Detail everything you are concerned about – then send it on to your boss and copy someone else, if you feel the need. By all means keep a copy of what you send.

Your boss will basically have two choices:

> To continue to ignore his responsibilities, and hence, you, in the communication loop

> Respond with what he actually wants, means, etc.

If the former, you now have documentation of how you interpreted things and thus a foundation to act upon and to stand up on.

The Technique you need to Learn NOW

Great memos for difficult bosses (Useful in dealing with all bosses!)

Focus: Within one sentence your boss should know what this memo (e-mail) is about. This can include the title (subject line of an e-mail) AND the first sentence of the memo.

For Example:

> Subject: Eisenwasher contract update

First sentence/phrase:

FYI the Eisenwasher contract is two days ahead of the original projected completion date.

Short, terse, brief: Brief is almost always appreciated. Find the most succinct way to say what needs to be said. Ask this question, "What do I need to convey?"

E.g. FYI the Eisenwasher contract is two days ahead of planned schedule:

Don has preliminary data worked up and is working on Phase II

Sally is done with the legal description. I will review today.

Steve has financial outlay information ready and is checking on several new vendors for cost-savings potential.

I will send another update by the end of the week. We should have the contract ready to send to you for final approval by next Thursday.

Let me know if you need any more info. I am always ready to help out.

Hope your day is going well, Joe

To the point: There is nothing extra here. If you need to discuss something else or inform your boss of another issue, send another terse memo. Anything added will lessen the impact of this memo and when things start to get cluttered, the attention drifts quickly.

Repeating that important rule of thumb: stick to one issue per e-mail or memo

Ask yourself, "Can Don read this at a glance, i.e. within two minutes?" (preferably less than one minute!) Anything longer and it might be tabled or ignored.

Outline: An outline of key ideas is a great way to approach any memo or e-mail:

It helps you get organized.

It can be very helpful in keeping things succinct and to the point.

It is easy for someone to focus on key points.

Your outline may be all you need other than an introductory sentence or two.

Keep the memo: Having a disk of ALL the work relevant e-mails and memos you send is a VERY wise thing to do. It covers your backside, which, believe me, your difficult boss isn't going to do because he is too busy covering his. It gives you a paper trail of everything important that transpires on any given issue in case you need to revisit something for any reason.

If the news is not good: When you have to deliver bad news, be proactive and solution-oriented:

> "We didn't get the Frist contract, Bob. I'm following this up with them to determine what were the deciding factors so we can be more competitive next quarter. Let me know if you have any thoughts on how I should approach this issue."

Use the bad news opportunity to suggest proactive ways to help you and others learn from the experience.

If you need a response, more information, guidance

Don't demand: ask kindly, suggest, find ways to phrase things so that the information you need from your boss is in his best interest to give you:

> "John, your input on these data is very important to our success with this project. You have the expertise and eye to really make a difference, and I think if we could meet with you briefly, that would be all the catalyst we need to get high marks on this from above."

Be Positive as well as Professional

So much of what we write about and communicate in the business world is, well, business. Take some time at least once or twice a week to put some positivity in the mail:

Accomplishments:

Of your team

Of colleagues

Of yourself: "Ben, I just nailed the Johnson bid, thought you'd want to know right away."

Good things that happen, business-wise or personal:

"Hey, everyone, John's wife just had an eight pound, two ounce baby boy."

"Everyone finished the Royce seminar, that makes 100% compliance for the team."

NEVER!

Be evasive; beat-around-the-bush

Be dishonest

Offer excuses – it shows weakness – unless you are specifically asked for an explanation. Then keep it professional and non-blaming. Take responsibility if you should and offer to help find solutions.

ALWAYS!

Stay alert for ways to facilitate information flow with your boss and colleagues.

The more comfortable everyone is in sharing information the more information will be shared. Someone has to keep the door open to start with.

Open, positive communications are the best means to accomplish this

Set a positive example through your own efforts. Being forthright and open with your colleagues is as important as providing information for your boss. Your boss may initially set the stage for interoffice communications and negative information flow, but there is no reason it has to stay that way. You CAN make a major difference by working with everyone.

Keep in mind: that there are always more positive ways we can communicate with others. It takes practice and mental alertness to keep on top of this.

ASK! (Again!)

Poor information flow from above is unfortunately one of the most prevalent BAD business/managerial practices today. Sometimes it is caused by managers being too busy, forgetful, or stressed themselves, but far too often it is caused by neglect, poor leadership, 'broken' information flow patterns, and everyone playing things close-to-the-chest. Far too often there is no reason for such poor communications down the chain.

Most of the time, it doesn't hurt to ask.

In difficult times, especially when overworked, stressed, or times of change, etc., if you have the chutzpah, you can approach your boss and request more information.

> "Paul, I know there are things that are typically kept under wraps, but I really feel it would help the team if the administration were willing to provide a bit more upfront information about what is happening. People are getting really antsy and depressed out on the floor and I think productivity is sliding because everyone is so worried about what might happen. Do you think it is possible that we could be better informed?"

Questions and Ideas for Contemplation

There is a great deal you can do for yourself through good, solid communications and information sharing. When you start to consider the ramifications and possibilities of the knowledge in this chapter, you will see the doors it can start to open for you. Try some of these skills out over the next few weeks and see how it affects your own attitude at work and the attitudes of your boss and colleagues:

Over communicate

Take lots of notes

Send terse, professional memos/e-mails

Make every effort to keep people informed, even if they are on-the-periphery.

Always keep in mind: almost everyone likes to be informed and to be kept informed!

Chapter 18

WHO'S IN CONTROL?

"Don't take it personally. Most of the time another person's difficultness isn't about you.

When someone is difficult it is always a reflection of his innermost state." (Sandra Crowe)

Control Issues

Perceived control is a major issue in all toxic relationships. People placed in managerial and leadership roles naturally feel, as a result of their position, that they should have a certain amount of power and control over their realm. The difference between a leader and a person who only manages people is how they use that power:

> Is it with integrity?

> Are they honest with others?

> Do they accept responsibility for their work, for how they approach others, for success **and** failure?

> Do they take ownership of their own work and not others?

> Do they care?

> > For their employees?

> > The team?

> > The organization?

'Difficult' managers NEED to feel in control of others. It is how they overcome their own feelings of inadequacy, i.e. feeling they are not 'good enough.'

Give 'it' to them

Except for extreme misuses of power, control of others is largely an illusion. True control is self-control, which is now becoming a part of your repertoire of skills.

There is <u>nothing</u> to be gained from a power struggle

with your boss.

In reality we can almost always give up our need to be right and to feel in control of whatever it is we think we need to be in-control of (the situation? another person?), by maintaining our composure and working with our emotions, thoughts and reactions. Learn to be in control of yourself and you will be able to make a major difference in how your interactions go with a difficult person.

Keep in mind these key ideas from earlier in this book:

> **Reacting** to (difficulty, negativity, etc.) is giving over our control to another person.

> Choosing our **response** is maintaining our self-control and hence **staying in control of the situation from our own perspective**. This is what is most important.

> Allowing someone to be 'right' rarely causes us to give up anything and in the case of control freaks it helps them believe they are in control and 'right,' which is part of what drives their difficulty. Why fight battles that don't need to be fought?

You are difficult, too

Well, very likely you are difficult from their perspective.

Difficult people see the people they interact with as difficult. It is also quite likely that they assume that you are capable of the same types of difficult behaviors, power trips, and controlling behaviors they are, even though you are not like them at all.

Don't assume that your boss understands who you are, what you are about, and what you are doing. Tell him/her. But be sure to always be brief and direct. Good bosses try to know what is going on with their reports, but it is never that easy. They are busy, too. Lousy bosses may not care, but you can still make sure they know.

It pays to be upfront about who you are and what is important to you. I tell my clients to SAY IT:

> "That is a good point, Jim, and I appreciate your openness. I really believe we need to be open and honest with each other in order to have the best team possible." (Good to say even if they haven't been open and honest.)

> "You are right, Joan, quality is very important. I try every day to make sure I get things right. I will make every effort to get it right the first time, but if I make a mistake, be assured I will get on it right away. I appreciate your keeping me on my toes. (This is a great speech for a 'critical' boss.)

> "You know me, Dick, I try to stay as positive as possible. Be sure to kick-start me, if I begin getting negative around here." (Good thing to say to a very negative boss. He might begin to understand how negative he's been.)

> "Nell, I want you to know that I will always stay on top of things here and will make sure our projects move along. I will keep you apprised of progress on a daily basis." [Important for a 'Get-it-done,' micromanaging boss.]

There are many opportunities almost every day to let people know where you stand and what you hold dear. Use them. People may not understand the first time, or second, or...but if you keep at it, they may start get the point.

Blame

"The problem is we end up basing our well-being on someone else's behavior.... Our feelings are dictated by their behaviors, behaviors over which we have little or no control." (Rosen)

We all make mistakes. Though we wish we could be perfect and though we probably strive to make our lives and our work lives the best we can, we don't always live up to our ideals. Difficult bosses often use blame as a means of control and power.

You NEVER need to accept someone else's blaming you

as a measure of your **self-worth**.

Yes, there are times when we should apologize because we erred or could have done better. That does not mean we have to accept being 'beaten up' by our boss or by ourselves (with negative thinking and disparaging self-talk). It does mean we should take responsibility and ownership for what we have done, learn from our experiences, and move ahead proactively by being solution oriented.

How to approach a 'blaming' boss

If you did make a mistake:

> "Ted, you are right. I'm sorry, I should have seen this coming, but I didn't. I accept full responsibility and will make a sincere effort to turn this around. I appreciate your pointing this out. That way I can learn from my mistakes."

Apologize; accept responsibility for what you did or didn't do; suggest a follow-up and if feasible specifics aimed at a solution. Don't back down. cringe, fight back, or dwell excessively on the situation with excessive guilt/worry. You are a stand-up, self-confident, pro-active employee who takes responsibility and gets things done. Offer no excuses unless specifically asked for an explanation. Then do so without assigning blame and maintaining your willingness to be responsible.

If you didn't make a mistake:

> "Ted, sorry about the mess. I'm not sure what happened or where this came from, but I will get right on finding a solution. Do you have any suggestions, or should I jump right in and see what I can do?"

Apologizing doesn't hurt. You are being responsible by showing you are willing to take action, though you are not accepting responsibility for what went wrong. You are also not assigning blame (very important) to anyone (including your boss, who may actually be the culprit). You are also not offering any excuses.

Pointing your finger at others weakens your team and it lessens your boss' perception of you. Ninety-nine percent of the time your boss will know who actually screwed up, even though they may not admit to it, nor accept the blame for their own mistakes.

Most difficult bosses, even those who tend to blame others, respect those who respect themselves and who are willing to take a 'let's deal with this' stance and attitude.

It is often the situation; not you

Many difficult behaviors are manifested because the 'difficult' person is stressed and unable to handle their own feelings and thoughts. You just happen to be there and available.

Part of the reason that difficult bosses are so successful at being difficult is because we ARE available. We react and act just the way they expect us to. Change how we react to their behavior and we change the whole dynamics of the situation. Understanding how we contribute to (make ourselves 'available' to) a difficult boss' behavior really makes a difference in our eventual success in dealing with that person's behavior(s).

All those difficult bosses

There are as many types of difficult bosses

as there are difficult bosses.

This is an important concept to wrap your understanding around. While we will list a variety of categories of difficult bosses in the next chapter and discuss them in subsequent chapters of this book, the truth is, no one fits perfectly into a type, label, or category. YOU are the best judge the types of difficult behaviors you have to deal with. The following exercise is KEY to your success with them.

Know the behaviors

The best way to succeed with difficult bosses is discussed in all the fundamental ideas presented to this point in this book. Many difficult people will change their interactions/difficult behaviors with you **because you have changed your approach to them** by being more self-aware, self-confident, positive, open, honest, kind, etc. However, we often still have to deal with long-ingrained behavior patterns that these difficult individuals use. Start the rest of your quest to succeed with your difficult boss by delineating these behaviors as specifically as possible.

Answer this question:

> My boss upsets/irritates/'gets to me' because he/she...

List a specific behavior that bothers you, e.g.

> She explodes over nothing, and if I'm within range, I'm the one caught in the line of fire.

Then specify exactly how she manifests this behavior:

She usually throws open her door, glares around the room, stalks over to my desk and starts hollering. Half the time I can't tell what she is yelling about and I have no clue as to why I'm the one she usually picks on. Most of the time, when I finally understand what she is saying through the curse words and negativity, it isn't about me or anything I did, but I end up feeling guilty and...

Next, describe your typical thoughts, feelings, and your usual reaction to this outburst.

...I end up feeling guilty, ashamed, even though I haven't done anything wrong. I get red in the face and I can feel myself flinching and shrinking lower into my chair. I lower my eyes and just sit there nodding. I feel awful, my stomach is in knots, I can hardly stammer out any words, which usually end up being, "I'm sorry," or some sort of wimpy response. I keep thinking, "Why me?" "What did I do wrong?" "Why do I have to put up with this?" and so on. Later I feel wiped out, totally drained and really embarrassed around my fellow workers. I shrink home with my tail between my legs and end up being depressed for a long time.

Then describe her reaction to what you do.

After her tirade runs itself out, she just glares at me and usually turns away in a huff. Later that day or the next day she will come out and be as pleasant as the next person to me. Like nothing has happened. Then I feel confused and even more depressed. I just don't know how to deal with this. I feel lost.

This person can be hard to deal with at first because the situation you are facing and the behavior(s) you are dealing with may be very emotionally charged. Stick to your guns and try to do this technique of specifying the behavior, situation, and your reactions for any and all different types of negative/difficult behaviors and situations you feel you have to work through. The more specific you can be, the better.

You are accomplishing a number of very important things with this exercise:

You are facing some of your demons – the behaviors that push your buttons.

You are acknowledging how you feel, think, and react.

You are stepping back and really looking at what is happening, which IS the first step to being able to deal with it in a different way. That pause, removed from the actual situation itself, gives you more self-control when this same behavior is perpetrated again.

You are looking more logically at what it is your boss does that bothers you. Making an effort to separate this from your immediate emotional reaction, changes the dynamics of the situation the next time it happens, thus clearing the way for changes you can make that will work better for you.

You are focusing on the behavior; not the person. Deal with the behavior and you can be successful; try to change the person and you won't get very far. [Most of us have tried that far too much, unsuccessfully!]

Do it!

This is one of those things we all tend to put off or find excuses not to do.

"I will do it later."

"I will think about it."

"I get it. No point in dragging myself through an exercise."

IF you have a difficult boss and you aren't being successful with their difficult behaviors, please do this exercise – in writing. It WILL be worth the time and effort!

I have written books, taken notes, kept journals my whole life and it is:

Cathartic

Eye-opening

Helps us reach even deeper than 'just thinking things through'

Helps us open our mind's eye and our creative thinking

Gives something concrete to read; something we can go through again, and revisit two, four, six months down the road as we improve our skills.

By all means take some long walks and think this through. That, coupled with this exercise can really help you see the whole range of things that contribute to your troubles.

Another hint: If you have a negative experience with your boss, see if you can find the time as soon thereafter to go through this exercise while the memories are fresh. It will give you further insight into what you put up with and what you go through.

Once you have done this, you have set yourself in a position where you can really bring everything to bear in using your knowledge, understanding, skills, and tools toward being successful with this difficult person.

Questions and Ideas for Contemplation

"You can't change other people...directly.

You can only change yourself." (Koob)

This book is about changing yourself and behaving differently in stressful situations so that as your difficult boss interacts with you, those personal changes effect change in him. Much of what follows in this text will be generic examples to show you the different ways in which your responses can make a big difference in how the dynamics of a given situation and ultimately the dynamics of your work life pan out.

Your task will be to take the specific information you have gathered about your boss' difficult behavior(s), and learn to apply the techniques and tools delineated throughout this text to any given situation in which you find yourself. When you can couple this approach with what you have learned and practiced from the first part of this book, you should be able to deal with almost anything that comes your way.

Chapter 19

DIFFICULT BOSSES

Many books and articles that discuss difficult people issues focus on a broad perspective that is somewhat all-inclusive. Even those that are work or business-focused tend to discuss a more generic approach, without considering the differences engendered by the **control** and **power** issues that are so important to being successful with difficult bosses. The next few chapters will include these critical considerations as the jumping off place for discussing difficult boss behaviors.

Characteristic Behaviors

"Some managers are toxic because they are clueless about their

effect on others...and some are toxic because they are simply

overwhelmed with stress." (Roy Lubit)

Aggressive Behaviors (Chapter 20)

Bosses can be very aggressive. With some people in power it seems to be almost the nature of the beast. When they want something done, or are upset because something, at least from their perspective, is not right, they can 'get-in-your-face' and use intimidation to get what they want.

Aggression can take many forms. The overriding principle is that we feel attacked or pushed by someone beyond what is our comfort level or what we feel would be normal boundaries. We can understand the aggressive boss through our own emotional reactions and through our perception of their emotions and reactions.

We may feel:

Angry

Frustrated

Defensive

Confused

Guilty/Ashamed

Shocked

Depressed

Or think that:

We are not-good-enough, inadequate, less than

What we think they are feeling/thinking:

Angry or upset with us

That we are to blame for whatever it is they are upset about

That we are incompetent, worthless, not-good-enough

That we are lazy

That we can't do anything right

As detailed in the previous chapter it is helpful for you to put these emotions and thoughts into your own words, by examining specific encounters you have had with your boss.

Dominating Behaviors (Chapter 21)

While aggressive bosses can seem quite dominating, the energy and effort of a domineering boss is to be in control of everything. He wants all the power. Nit-pickers, the highly critical, and especially micro-managers, who have to have their hands in everything, typify bosses who seem to be on our case day in and day out.

This type of behavior is very frustrating. We want to be able to prove our worth, but our boss keeps insinuating himself into every facet of our work life. He or she gives you responsibilities and leeway and then stands looking over your shoulder to make sure you don't screw up. Or worse yet, he goes ahead and makes the decisions and does some of the work before you have a chance to do anything.

Your frustrations are probably quite legitimate. However, it never pays to wallow in negativity. Detail the behaviors that bother you the most, and identify your frustrations as specifically as possible. One of the concerns in dealing with this type of behavior is that it is very difficult to get your boss to change his habits, so understanding how ingrained and pervasive this behavior is can be important to your success.

As you will see, by changing your behavior you can stay ahead of your boss and anticipate many of his concerns. Your ability to do this will help ease your frustrations, and in the long run can change the dynamics of your relationship with your boss as he begins to trust you more and more. He will still be who he is, i.e. concerned about details ad infinitum, but you will have shown him that you are on top of things and he won't have to be such a watchdog, at least in your camp.

Also, keep in mind how this type of behavior can be increasingly frustrating if you let it get to you. When you notice yourself starting to get anxious and uptight, it is time to step back and reevaluate and reorganize your strategies. You should also take some time to care for yourself. When you are feeling down or anxious, it is much harder to be positive, proactive, and kind.

Passive-Aggressive Behaviors (Also, see Chapter 22)

Bosses who do things indirectly and surreptitiously can be very disconcerting.

> I once had a boss who would tape negatively-laced memos to my door (this was before e-mail) because he couldn't actually face me with what he wanted to say. Even in end-of-year evaluations, I wouldn't know anything about how he felt about my work until I actually got the evaluation in my packet. If I asked him how I was doing he would say, 'Fine.'

Indirect aggressive types of behavior are very stressful to deal with. If you have a boss who talks negatively about you behind your back, sabotages or discredits your work through another colleague, works to foster opposition to your ideas by gathering votes outside of a key meeting, etc., you are dealing with someone who has a great deal of difficulty facing people. Unfortunately, these types are quite willing to work behind the scenes to get their way and to make sure they are in control.

We all want to be kept in the loop, and when you have to deal with a boss who tends to communicate or do things indirectly, it can be very frustrating. Establishing and maintaining communications and information flow is critical with this type of boss. You have to be committed to a positive, supportive approach in order to get this type of person to be willing to work with you directly.

Passive Behaviors (Chapter 25)

Some bosses just don't seem to do anything, or at least not from their employees' perspective. A passive boss might hide out in his office and almost never communicate with his team; he may refuse to make decisions and tell you to 'just handle it.' He may be unresponsive or resistant to any overtures, or any attempt to communicate. Or he could just be bored, indifferent, and apathetic to everything.

If you are hardworking and dedicated to your work life, you may feel like you end up making all the decisions for yourself, as well as a good many for the team. You may want to scream, because no matter what you try, your boss just doesn't seem to care or want to get involved. Passive bosses tend to take a good bit of TLC (tender-loving-care) to get them to begin to be involved and active. Your patience and kindness will be tested every day, but if you persevere you can make a difference. If you are assertive and in-control, you can go a long way toward manifesting your own destiny under this type of leadership.

Bosses with Serious Needs and Concerns (Chapter 27)

Occasionally in life we do end up working for/with a person who really does have some concerns that are beyond anything we should have to deal with. Your boss could have a serious mental, emotional, and/or physical problem that limits their ability to work effectively with others and to be an effective leader.

Please don't 'evaluate' or label your boss. That is a job for a professional. If things are very disconcerting and everything you have done doesn't seem to help, you can go to an appropriate department at your business and get help (Human Resources, legal department, etc.). If you want to be helpful and proactive, go with the idea that you want to help this person, and to make the best of a difficult situation for yourself, your team, and your business.

Please remember that kindness and compassion, coupled with a positive attitude can make a big difference, even if they don't completely solve your concerns. You are the only person who is able to evaluate the situation completely and make the right decision for YOURSELF.

REALLY Difficult Bosses

Yes, there are some bosses who are extremely difficult, set-in-their-ways, and about as curmudgeonly as they can get. But believe it or not, even they can be, and often are, approachable and changeable by the many ideas, skills, and tools presented in this book.

You may think you have the MOST difficult boss ever. But I am willing to bet that the dynamics of your relationship <u>can</u> change in a more positive and effective direction, if you stick with your program of self-awareness and self-control. Use 'The Seven Keys to Being Successful with Difficult People,' and persevere. It can take time. You have to be willing to pick yourself up and dust yourself off when the going gets tough, and get right back on track with your positive approach.

Legal Issues

There are bosses who either through ignorance or stupidity stretch the bounds of decency and acceptability in the workplace. There are ways to deal successfully with inappropriate, harassing behaviors. It is important to always stick up for your rights, and not accept any form of inappropriate behavior.

It is VERY important to immediately seek help if there are ever any safety concerns for you or anyone on your team.

If you feel you have been harassed in any way, it is important to deal with this immediately. (Chapter 29)

Descriptive Types of Difficult Behaviors

Below is a short list of behaviors that difficult people (bosses) can manifest. You could probably add to this list. We have all probably come in contact with some of these types in the course of our life and work.

Bosses who:

are dishonest

Backstab, manipulate

are Gossips, Rumor-mongers

are Obsequious

are Irritable, Short-tempered

are Bullies, Intimidating, Verbally abusive

are Inept, Unreliable

who won't Make a Decision, Unavailable, always say "No"

are Rigid, Set-in-their-ways

are Unmotivated

are Nitpickers, Perfectionists, Always Right

are Self-centered, Self-absorbed,

Whine, Complain, Blame

are Rude, Obnoxious

are Curmudgeons, Stubborn/Hard-headed

are Inappropriate, Harassing

IMPORTANT: Keep in mind: that how you approach difficulties (difficult people) makes all the difference. No matter how daunting the behavior, the skills and techniques you can learn and practice using this book, CAN work.

Questions and Ideas for Contemplation

There are many approaches to considering different difficult behaviors that bosses manifest in the workplace. Any technique we use will be limited because of the necessity to discuss generalities. Your task in working with your boss is to apply concepts discussed throughout this book to the difficult behaviors you have to deal with, so that you can ease the frustrations that have been so much a part of your relationship with them. This is why delineating, very specifically, the concerns you have with your boss, and the frustrations you experience, are so important. Your success may depend on it.

A great exercise would be to go through this extensive list of behaviors and to circle the ones that really seem to describe the concerns you have with your boss. This effort can give you some added perspective as you read through the rest of this book.

Please keep any materials you put in writing extremely confidential for your own and others safety.

Chapter 20

AGGRESSIVE BEHAVIORS

Dealing with Aggression

"Here he goes again!"

"Whoa!"

"Wait a minute. Where did this come from?"

"So much for a peaceful, easy day. She is on the rampage again."

Do these thoughts sound familiar when you find your boss is suddenly in your face and on your case?

Aggressive bosses need to be dealt with assertively

If you respond **defensively** or **aggressively** to your boss' aggression, the likely outcome will be an escalation of the stakes, AND you will probably be labeled in some way by your boss: as a troublemaker, instigator, and, quite possibly, as a difficult person.

If you have responded aggressively in any way to your boss' attacks in the past, what happened?

> Can you relive this type of experience and recognize how your reactions impacted the situation?

> How did your boss react to you?

> How did you feel afterward?

Gaining some perspective from these questions can be very important in starting anew with your boss using a different strategy.

If you respond **passive-aggressively,** i.e. you don't get directly aggressive with him, but make comments to other coworkers, complain, do things behind his back, etc., you can count on your boss hearing about it one way or another. He will then think of you as a: whiner, complainer, blamer, sneak, backstabber, etc.

If you look at your past behaviors reflective of your boss' aggressive nature, have you responded passive-aggressively?

Have you let out your frustrations and anger indirectly?

Self-awareness and your ability to be honest with yourself is a key to being able to get past these types of self-destructive behaviors.

If you tend to respond **passively** to your boss' aggression, i.e. you withdraw into yourself and don't react at all, you flinch, back away or run off, etc., your boss will very likely think less of you – he may think you are cowardly or wimpy, that you lack chutzpah, etc. Passive reactions to aggression can encourage your boss to continue his attacks, the way he treats you. He may see you as a willing, or at least, tolerating victim.

Choose assertiveness

Whatever way you have reacted in the past, it is probably time for a change. Aggressive bosses tend to respect those who are willing to stand up to them without being aggressive or defensive. It is possible to learn how to do this. You need to commit to changing your tactics with your boss, and you need to find the courage to remain calm and in-control despite anything they do.

Remaining in-control and not reacting outwardly is very important when dealing with an aggressive boss.

Keys to responding assertively to your boss' tirades

Stand (or sit) erect at a comfortable distance (if this is feasible), remain calm

Make eye contact without challenging your boss; try not to stare, look away, or look down. You don't have to hold their gaze indefinitely, but try to keep your eyes focused generally toward their face. Looking away or down for an extended period can denote fear, timidity, etc.

Keep your face relaxed and neutral, e.g. don't grimace, frown, or smile

Stay aware of both your physical and emotional responses to your boss' aggression. Also, remain alert for any change in his/her demeanor as the result of what you are doing. If his behavior seems to be escalating, try changing your demeanor slightly, until you find what seems to work best and is comfortable for you. [E.g. back up a bit; act like you are paying careful attention; look down for an instant and immediately back up; nod 'yes' to let him know you are 'with' him; relax your body/stance; etc.]

Responding

You can remain calm and alert without saying anything until the worst of their tirade runs down...or...

You can repeat their name several times to gain their attention:

"John...John...John...I'm listening; I'm here for you...."

It is important to let them know several things right from the start:

You ARE alert and paying attention to them (your body language will help with this).

You are ready and able to help them with their concern(s).

You are ready to help and to get things done.

You let them know that they don't have to scream to get your attention.

A Scenario

Your boss charges into your cubicle and starts yelling about the Johnson Contract. Initially you can't make out what she is specifically upset about, but you know that you and at least six other people in the office have worked on this document recently.

You sit quietly, erect but non-confrontationally and look directly at your boss without challenging her. Since she is obviously 'over-the-top', you decide to try to bring her out of her tirade as soon as possible by repeating her name. You keep your voice even, slightly louder than normal, but you don't try to match her volume. Use the following type of phraseology when you have the opportunity. Don't force it. It may take a few minutes to get it all in.

"Jean...Jean...I'm listening. I can see you are upset about the Johnson contract, but I can't understand what you are trying to tell me. Please calm down and I will make every effort to help you with this problem. I'm really sorry you are so upset. Whatever the problem is, I will make every effort to make it right."

You may not get all of this out at once and it may take a moment or two for Jean to calm down enough for either of you to move forward to an understanding and a solution, but go with the flow. Keep calm; stay with your self-confident approach. The most important point is that you don't react to her aggression. You handle it calmly because you know it is her and not you that currently has a problem, and because your self-control will make all the difference in how this scene works itself out.

At this point you should let her know that you are paying close attention to her needs and concerns and that you **understand that she is upset** (a very important element). You also should let her know that she doesn't have to yell to get your attention. You apologize, even though you don't have a clue as to who is at fault (a good tactic that doesn't mean you accept any blame, you are simply being compassionate), and you let her know you are ready to do something about the problem.

Once you have her attention and she calms down, you should **listen carefully** to everything she has to say. Use good listening skills, pay attention, respond with nods, "Yes,' 'Uh-huhs,' etc., and **paraphrase** back to her key points if/when you have the opportunity. If you feel it will help, and it very well might, take out a notebook and jot down key ideas. This shows you really do want to make a difference and are trying to help. It also acknowledges the importance of her concern to you.

Find ways to be supportive, encouraging, solution-oriented.

"Jean, I appreciate what you have told me. I will do everything I can to ensure that this problem is addressed. I want you to know that I will be here for you. All you have to do is give me a jingle and I will tackle whatever it is you are concerned about."

You are reinforcing everything that went before and indirectly you are letting her know that her explosions aren't necessary. It also makes good sense to throw in a compliment, 'thanks,' something positive. You are being proactive about seeing that the problem is addressed, but you are not accepting responsibility for creating it, nor do you necessarily have to shoulder the whole burden. You are, however, going to get the ball rolling.

"Thanks, Jean. I understand much more than I did before. You have really thought this through and I know we can make this contract better with your input."

It doesn't hurt to be upbeat, positive, supportive, and complimentary at the end.

Finally, be willing to return to something key for you: telling her how you feel about her approach.

Do this when you feel comfortable doing so, and when the timing seems right, typically after her aggression, anger, and frustration have run their course and she has calmed. [Hint: you may want to do this on another occasion when she is calm and focused and in a better mood.]

> "Jean, I just wanted to let you know that I understand how frustrating your work can be and that I am here to help in any way that I can. It would help me to help you, if you could just come and get me when something is building up so that we can deal with all of this calmly. I would appreciate it very much if we could just talk things through. Thanks."

IMPORTANT

Most aggressive bosses will respond fairly quickly to this type of focused approach. You may have to put up with one or two more explosions, but it would be very unusual for your boss not to be affected by your positive, in-control approach.

The most important ideas represented here get right at your aggressive boss' 'difficult' behaviors:

> You are being attentive without being aggressive or wimpy

> You are being supportive and appreciative

> You are willing to make a difference -- get-it-right, get it done; help to fulfill her needs, wants, and desires.

> You are non-judgmental, but willing to take a stand about how you like to be approached.

A Step Beyond: Another way to say it

On rare occasions you may have to take one further step, especially if you discussed this earlier with her or if she didn't 'get it' the first time. On a day when your boss is calm, and perhaps in a slightly better mood than normal, it is okay to be assertive and ask her for a moment to talk about something concerning you. Then be willing to broach this delicate subject:

> "Jean, you are a great boss and have a great knowledge base in this field. I really respect your work and leadership. I am trying very hard to live up to your impeccable standards. One thing that concerns me, though, is that I feel very uncomfortable when you get so upset when something goes wrong.

> "I want you to know that I am here for you and that I will listen carefully anytime you need me. I would like us to be able to have a relationship in which we can discuss everything calmly and openly. Is there anything else I can do to help our interactions remain on an even keel throughout the day?"

Say it!

It does take courage to be assertive, and it takes control to stand up to someone who is very aggressive. However, I am a firm believer in open communication. It is often far better to get something irritating out in the open so that two grownups can deal with it directly, than to let things fester because her behavior doesn't change.

When you feel you have to talk over an uncomfortable situation or problem with a difficult, aggressive boss, you must be willing to take the plunge. Make sure you are prepared. It is a good idea to plan out, in detail, what you want to say so that you find the most positive, supportive way to say it. If you feel you have trouble doing this, you can get help from a qualified coach or mentor. Just keep in mind that:

There are always positive ways to approach concerns

and difficulties...

ways that are self-supportive and supportive of others.

When you begin to learn how to do this, it will make a major difference in your communications with your boss. It could make all the difference in your comfort and energy levels at work, too.

Paying Attention

At the root of working with aggressive personalities is a very key idea:

They need to know that you are paying attention to them.

When you offer this type of close attention, they will almost always respond more positively and begin to change their behavior toward you.

Paying attention is so important because it:

> Shows them that what they say is important to you
>
> Acknowledges them for who they are
>
> Shows appreciation
>
> Shows concern
>
> Is a form of recognition

Positive attention can assuage even the most savage 'beast'. Sometimes all we really need is someone to pay attention to us. Keep this important point in mind with all difficult boss behaviors.

Keep in Mind

It is important to know your boss (see Chapter 9). The better you understand how they interpret and approach things the better you can temper your communications and approach to elicit change. What may work well with one boss, may not be the best approach with another. Try different things. Be willing to adjust as necessary to a difficult situation.

Questions and Ideas for Contemplation

There are many different forms of aggression in the workplace. Positive, assertive, proactive, solution-oriented approaches will often work well with many different boss types. Use your best judgment in any given situation – your best understanding of who your boss is and how they may respond to you and what you do. Make sure that your safety and the safety of others is of paramount concern.

Plan, practice, re-practice scenarios before you approach your boss. The better prepared you are, the less likely it will be that you will return to old reactions, and the more likely that you will make positive choices that work.

The predominant **intent** of an aggressive boss:

Probably to 'get it done,' and quite possibly, 'to get it right.'

His **needs**: a sense of power over others which helps to mitigate his feelings of inferiority.

What he **wants**: your attention

What he **desires/cares about**: being accepted [Hard to believe, but true!]

Chapter 21

DOMINATING BEHAVIORS

Hyper-critical, Micro-managing, "I'm always right'

Power and Control are major issues for most difficult boss types. They seem to be at the forefront of behaviors that make us feel like we have been overly controlled, highly criticized, or pushed into areas and directions that are uncomfortable for us.

Succeeding with bosses who exhibit these behaviors means we work within our own self-confident, self-controlled stance and let our difficult boss manage their own control and power issues. We can choose to let their behavior bother us, or we can make more positive choices for ourselves. Our personal approach is critical.

Perfectionists

Some bosses seem to be almost impossible to please. If you write a terrific fifty-page document, they will manage to find the two typos in it, and that is what they will focus on and let you know about. No matter what we do, they seem to be able to find fault. Far too often, we let their criticism weigh us down until our work just doesn't seem worth the effort to do.

Micro-managers

Perfectionist behavior and the need to make sure everything is done right, go hand and hand. Micro-managers make assignments and offer responsibility, and then stand over you day in and day out to make sure you get it right. In worst-case scenarios they may go behind your back and do the task themselves because they just can't leave things to chance. If you work for a micro-manager, you may feel used, impotent, oppressed, paranoid, etc.

There is hope

While perfectionist bosses and micro-managers can be very difficult to deal with and even harder to succeed under, it is possible to make a major difference in how you feel about your job and about yourself – by making positive changes in your approach to your work.

At the outset

There are two key issues in being successful with perfectionist and micromanaging behaviors:

Being the best you can be (and letting them know that is what you strive for)

Keeping them informed at every step of the way

Being the BEST

Doing the best you can, every moment you are at work, may be something you already strive for, but it may not be enough,' for your hypercritical boss. It may never be enough, but there are ways to make your efforts recognized, less criticized, and more appreciated:

Make a commitment, regardless of your boss' reactions, to do everything in your power to 'get things right.' This is their modus operandi; almost, it seems, their reason for being.

Not only get-it-right but let them know, fairly often, that getting it right and top quality are also very important to you. You have to say it:

> "Harry, I have the contract ready to go. I have been through it carefully and have tried to make sure it is in the best shape possible. I know you have a keen eye, so let me know if there is anything that needs fixing. I want this to be top-of-the-line before we send it on. You know I always care about getting things right. I appreciate your input."

This technique gets things right out in the open and you are setting yourself up for his input. The interesting thing is that with this approach Harry is more likely to take things in hand with far less demonstrative criticism, because you have been upfront with wanting this to be perfect. Thanking them in advance for their input gets things out in the open, so that whatever they say is likely to be a whole lot less volatile from both the giving end and your receiving end because you have anticipated it. In addition, you have acknowledged their need and complimented them to boot.

Do your best:

Check, re-check, re-re-check your work

Read through on the computer; use a spell checker, thesaurus and grammar checker.

Read through a hard copy by getting it off the screen. The change in perspective often makes a difference in what you see.

Get help with drafts, even if you have to pay someone. This is especially critical if you are more of a 'get-it-done' person and not strong on details. Use your strengths; get help with your weaknesses!

Check it again.

Thank them for their criticism

If you still get criticism in spite of your best efforts, which is highly likely with this type of personality, thank them. They probably have found the one error in that twenty-page report, so they are 'right.' When you thank them, you release the power this incident has to upset you and you release your need to be right. Let it go and let them know you appreciate that they are so good at making things perfect. This plugs into their need for power, control, and appreciation, and it very well may help change the overall dynamics of your relationship over time.

Move ahead. Sometimes we have to make decisions that are forward looking for everyone's sake.

> I once had a boss who changed everything I wrote, every time I sent it up. The process would have never ended, even though after a while he would start changing things back to the way I had ha them in earlier 'corrected' versions. Ultimately, I learned that I had to take the bull by the horns and move that project ahead. I would write him a memo and say, "Dick, I think we have got this just right. I'm going to send it up to Bob later today after I make these last corrections. Let me know if there are any problems with anything by four o'clock." I never had any complaint from Dick, either. He was probably tired of this back and forth game too, but he just HAD to change things. It was his personality. Sometimes the right choice is to use your best judgment, but always keep your boss informed and up to date of what you plan to do.

Keeping them informed

The best technique besides getting things as right or perfect as possible with perfectionist bosses, and especially with micro-managers, is positive information flow:

Keep them informed and keep it coming.

Micro-managers are fearful that you won't get the work done, and won't get the work done right. Some can be so paranoid that they won't even give you a reasonable amount of time to get anything accomplished before they jump in and do it themselves.

Use the NOW technique

Just got an assignment from your micro-managing boss?

Run, don't walk, back to your office and send an immediate e-mail (or call) and tell him you are already on top of this and let him know what you are going to do right now, today, and what you will do within x-period of time. Delineate, specify, get it down on paper, let him know, NOW!

> Keep it brief
>
> High-light key points (especially if written in paragraph form)
>
> Outline or bullet key ideas
>
> Detail what you are doing, plan to do, and when
>
> Follow-up with frequent messages about how things are progressing

HINT! It is almost impossible to over-communicate with and/or over-inform these types of bosses. If you don't keep them informed, life will get very frustrating.

Important: frequent, short, to-the-point e-mails are best. Always keep the e-mail stream as back-up for possible reference and to refresh your own memory. Store them all on a disk for posterity. [See Chapter 17, "Information," for an example of an informative, short e-mail/memo.]

Keep it positive

> "John, I knew you would want to be kept abreast, so here is the latest data. I am staying on top of everything. Let me know if you need anything more from me. Everyone is up to speed on this one. We appreciate your input."
>
> "John, here is the e-mail I just received from legal. They are moving ahead and we are on track to get this done early."

Bad news: It is just as important to keep your boss informed of drawbacks and concerns. They are going to find out anyway. Might as well let them know AND, let them know what you are doing about it. Being proactive and solution-oriented is imperative.

> "Nina, the widget machine on Line 8 broke down at 2:55. This is going to put a crimp in our plans to get 100,000 doohickeys out by Monday morning. I am keeping up on this as it develops. The machine is currently being repaired. Here are some suggestions for making up for lost time..."

Informative, brief, taking responsibility, working toward a solution, getting things back on track – this type of response helps keep Nina off your back by keeping her informed about what is happening. Keep her informed at every juncture of progress or problems.

I'm ALWAYS Right (and you are wrong!)/ 'NO!' Bosses

There are definitely difficult bosses who seem to not only need their hand in everything but absolutely need to feel that it is 'their way or the highway.' It seems that no matter how you broach things to them, they won't listen to you, and if, on the rare occasion they do listen, their decisions completely ignore any advice you shared. They tend to dominate meetings, and push anyone and everyone to get their way. Even when they are obviously wrong, or the decision they made was obviously wrong, they simply ignore the facts and move on as if nothing happened. You and your colleagues will likely have to take the brunt of the fallout.

In worst cases a really difficult, 'always right,' boss may blame you or others for their foibles and mistakes – another good reason for information flow and documentation.

It seems that being wrong is something their inflated egos just cannot accept.

> Hint: It NEVER is a good idea to prove an 'always right' boss, 'wrong.'

Help them be right

All the advice given above in this chapter can also apply: keep them informed, keep it positive, and make sure you have all of your ducks in a row

Letting your boss be right most, if not all of the time, is not as difficult as it might seem. First, you have to give up your need to be right. As stated earlier in this book, most of the time being right is not that important. When it is important, help them be part of your 'rightness.'

Helping them be right without giving up anything

Get them involved in your ideas:

> "Beth, something you said the other day made me think of this approach. Take a look at this proposal and see how it fits in with your perspective. I think you will see that it works well and it jumps right off from what you suggested."

There doesn't have to be any specific thing that they said or did, just suggest they did and get them involved. It is smart politics to find ways to empower them. Find ways to tie in their approach/ideas with yours. Give them the opportunity to have a piece of the pie even if this is all or mostly yours.

Help them be a part of the idea

> "I think you will like this idea, Beth, but we need your expertise and wisdom to move this out of the planning stage. I know you will see ways we can implement this. I always appreciate your willingness to help kick my meanderings into high gear."

> "Beth, I really like your thoughts on this and it ties right in with what we have been doing. If we bring these two camps together under your guidance, I'm sure the administrative leaders will be very pleased."

Key point: A good approach is to insinuate that their boss will be pleased with what you are proposing. Your 'Always Right,' 'No' boss may think twice about nixing something the higher ups may like to see done.

In other words, feed their egos; feed their needs.

Get back to basics with these boss types. Your behavior can make a major difference:

> Thank them

> Appreciate their work, input, expertise

> Acknowledge their input and ability

> Recognize them for their contributions

Use good, basic, positive communications

Make a BIG DEAL of their involvement and contributions. Using these techniques and being on top of this type of approach from the start can eliminate a great deal of frustration. You already know the brick wall exists; there is no sense beating your head against it, and there are almost always positive ways around or over it.

Plan, plan, plan, and think things through. You will soon surprise yourself with your ingenuity for creating ways to move new ideas forward.

Taking care of YOU

Nitpickers, micromanagers, "always right,' bosses can quickly drain our energy levels and self-worth IF WE LET THEM. Your positivity throughout is important to your well-being. Their behavior is their own, and while it can be frustrating, especially when it seems to come from left field when we are not ready for it, we can quickly regroup and get back to solid footing by using these different skills and techniques.

Remind yourself every day of your own value. Other people don't determine whether you are good enough, YOU do.

Questions and Ideas for Contemplation

Perfectionist bosses will not change their tune because of the tactics discussed in this chapter. **They will, however,** likely change their overall approach to you and even appreciate you better for who you are and for your work. Often, they will still be critical. It is how they deal with the world, and you are not likely to change that. The important thing is for you to be able to work within parameters that are important to you, and that you are able to maintain your self-worth in spite of their behavior. Being proactive, solution-oriented, while firmly establishing positive information flow should help you to do this.

Keep in mind that when we deal with difficult bosses that a key concept is to attempt to give them what they need and want, while at the same time maintaining our own dignity, self-worth, and positivity. There are never any reasons we should have to give up the values and qualities we want to exemplify in our life and work.

The predominant **intent** of perfectionists, micromanagers, 'I'm always right' bosses:

Is to 'get things right.'

What they **need**: freedom from fear, anxiety, and failure.

What they **want**: for you to get it right; to feel in control.

What they **desire/care** about: being appreciated for what they feel is important; to have all their employees as quality-minded as they are.

Chapter 22

PASSIVE-AGGRESSIVE BEHAVIORS

Fear

Bosses who do things behind their employees' backs, or who find it difficult, if not impossible, to work with people face-to-face, often use indirect means to deal with others. It seems highly unethical, and certainly cowardly, to the person who has to work with such a boss. These behaviors are far more common than we might think. Additionally, some otherwise excellent managers might be very reluctant to deal with an employee face-to-face when they have something difficult or negative to impart.

Unfortunately, if your boss does not communicate well, and fails to keep you and other team members informed, you can feel like there are things going on behind the scenes. It doesn't take much surreptitious behavior in an office environment for everyone to start looking over their shoulders. Soon everyone is clamming up, keeping information to themselves, and finding less than open and honest means to get what they want.

Passive-aggressive behaviors include gossiping, back-stabbing, subterfuge and lying, manipulating, sabotaging, resistant, and vindictive types of behaviors. They can be very hard to deal with because they are well-buried under layers of bureaucracy and secrecy. Even when one can prove a deceptive approach has been used by a person in an authority position, it is even harder for a win-win outcome to a problem.

Get it Out in the Open

While we can spend a huge amount of effort and psychological energy garnering evidence and proving that our boss is a liar, cheat, back-stabber, or fundamentally unethical, we will have a far greater chance of success if we can deal with the issue directly ourselves. and there are ways to do this without creating an impossible job situation with no chance of comfort, advancement, or promotion.

Let them know you know

You can let your boss know you are on to their back-handed ways without directly accusing them. You have to let the 'rightness' issue slide and broach them as positively as possible:

"Carl, I have heard through the grapevine that someone was spreading rumors about my not having put much time in on the Jones Contract. I know you know how much work I did on that, so I'm counting on you to support my efforts as you know I support everything you do."

"Ann, someone seems to be working behind my back to sabotage my ideas for the Kensington Project. Since much of the work I have done comes from ideas you and I have discussed, I was hoping we could sit down and make sure we are on the same page with where this is headed. I appreciate all your attention on this as I know the project is one you want to see succeed."

There is no blame here and your primary aim is to get things out on the table. Throwing in a few kudos and supportive statements along the way is smart business, which can allow your boss to backpedal and ultimately to find a way to work things through with you without letting this concern go by the wayside or to escalate.

You can bring your concern out in the open at a meeting or through e-mail:

"I just wanted to check with everyone on where we stand with the Kensington Project. I have been hearing some rumors about some discontent, so I thought we could take a few minutes to chat about this before we get any deeper. I'm open to everyone's suggestions and input. Ann, maybe you would like to give us an overview of your perspective of where we are currently with this project to kick this off."

Again, you can do this with no finger-pointing and you are simply providing a forum to get things out on the table.

Ask:

"Ann, I am concerned about where the Kensington project is sitting. I would really like your thoughts on this so we are both on the same page. I respect your knowledge about this sort of plan and it would help me a lot to have you comment on my ideas as well as giving your own."

Open doors

By opening doors without blame or rancor you are capable of moving through difficulties and disagreements. If you get angry and defensive because you are suspicious of your boss' activities behind your back, even if you have certain proof of their deception, you create ill-will and a huge roadblock to progress. Your aim is not to be **right**, but to have a positive, quality, viable place to work.

Keep in mind that to succeed with a difficult boss you shouldn't aim at changing them, a nearly impossible task. You should aim at changing how they interact with you and how they treat you.

Each time you open eyes and doors by bringing things into the open, there is less of a likelihood that your boss is going to keep trying the same tactics in the future. However, change takes time and long habits are hard to break, so you may have to use this technique a number of times to make sure things aren't getting back to normal in an environment where surreptitious behavior has been the standard procedure for some time.

If any fellow employees have taken up your boss' mantle of negative behavior, use the same skills and tactics with them to keep things out in the open. It is hard for subterfuge and deception to thrive in an environment where one or more people insist on keeping things upfront and honest.

Information flow

As detailed in the previous chapter and Chapter 17 the flow of information to your boss (and colleagues) is critical for success. You can open doors and keep them open by creating an information flow that doesn't allow for much subterfuge:

> "I wanted to e-mail everyone the details of the Kensington project to date. Bulleted below are the key sticking points. Please review and send me your comments by the 16th. I have asked for a half hour at the weekly team meeting on the 18th for further discussion based on your responses. Ann and I will field questions at that time. If you want your input heard, please respond ASAP. Ted, Jamie, Glen, and Alexis input from your teams is critical to this moving ahead. I will check with each of you individually this week to follow up. Thanking you in advance for your prompt attention."

Information creates documentation. It isn't so much that you will need the documentation, but that everyone who gets this memo will know that everyone else got this memo. Whatever you have documented, is now common knowledge. It brings things out and allows for open discussion.

> Keep it professional

> Keep it brief

Keep it to the point

Thank everyone

Be positive wherever feasible

Don't blame, finger point, or complain

Let them know what you stand for: Say it!

If someone is lying to you, let them know you stand for honesty and openness.

> "Jan, I appreciate your openness. I am totally committed to an honest and open office environment."

If someone is gossiping, let them know that you believe in talking with people directly.

> "Frank, I don't know if what you said is true or not, but I think we should talk with Ionia about it, since she is the person involved. Do you want me to give her a call?"

> Frank will get the point immediately. He is likely to backpedal rapidly, deciding that talking with Ionia is unnecessary. It doesn't typically take more than a couple of neutral responses like this for someone to get the idea that you don't like to talk behind other people's backs.

Keep your ear to the ground

Paying attention to the dynamics in an office is smart business, especially if the general tenor has been for things to be handled under the table. It is a common reaction by a person or persons who are used to a certain method of operation to try to continue with it, perhaps at an even more secretive, deeper level. Stick to you guns of getting things out in the open and keeping them there.

IMPORTANT – As you develop your skills you can begin to anticipate possible concerns by opening up issues from the get-go. The more people in the know and the wider the door is opened, the less chance there is for clandestine meetings and hidden agendas.

Document

Keeping close tabs on all information that flows in and out of your box is good for you and good for keeping things open and honest. It can help you refresh your memory if you need to backtrack, and if it is widely known that you keep records of everything, it is less likely for people to try to put one over on you or try to put one 'by' you.

Resistant Behavior

Resistant behavior from your boss can include:

> Saying 'No' to everyone else's ideas
>
> Ignoring ideas even if they listen to them
>
> Doing what they want in spite of everyone else's wishes
>
> Sabotaging
>
> Scheming/Wheeling-dealing
>
> Being defensive
>
> Won't make decisions
>
> Unavailable/Unresponsive
>
> Rigid/Set-in-their-ways
>
> Stubborn/Hard-headed

Some bosses are resistant to almost anything different and/or to ideas that aren't their own (see previous chapter's section on 'Always Right' behavior). An obstructionist or "No" boss can be very frustrating to deal with.

Many of the ideas suggested with "Always Right" bosses are applicable here. Getting the resistant boss on board the team's ideas by helping them be engaged is one positive approach that can work fairly well. However, there are obstructionist bosses who just won't budge from the status quo or from 'that is the way we have always done it around here.'

The horns of a dilemma

I worked for many years for a "No" boss. He was very traditional and didn't seem to like new ideas or change. Whenever I broached him with a new creative idea for my team, he had some reason why it could not or should not be done. In looking back, I feel that this guy felt threatened by anything that was different, both because he thought there was a chance of failure and because I don't think he wanted others to be successful. He was also worried, from his perspective, that it might make him look bad.

I was not satisfied with the status quo and I decided fairly early on that if I was to enjoy my work, I wanted to make a difference. For me that meant using my creativity and intelligence to make things happen.

Just do it?

In those days I was young and pretty brash. I soon learned that if I wanted to accomplish the things that were important to me, I had to just do them. I put my energy into devising my plans, setting everything up, and moving ahead without letting my boss know what I was up to, instead of trying fruitlessly to convince him my ideas were sound. By the time I let the cat out of the bag, it was too late for him to say, "No!"

Was this the smart play?

Probably not, at least not entirely.

If I had been willing to get him on board by helping him be a part of my ideas and part of the planning and development, I may have had more success with him in the long run. In looking back, I may have won many small battles, but I probably lost some wars **because** I didn't consult him or get him involved. Unfortunately, I didn't have this understanding and these skills back then. Sometimes it is a difficult choice to make.

> My advice: when you can get your boss on the bandwagon, it IS the best approach. Much of the time, it is possible. Get creative in finding ways to get your boss involved!

Sometimes you have to find the balance point between doing what is important to you at the time and being smart about your relationship with your boss. Your boss is/may be a key person for your future success. Finding ways to work within his shortcomings, while at the same time being able to move ahead with what is important to you, are the best long-term tactics.

141

It takes:

> Knowing your boss

> Finesse

> Positivity

> Compromise

> Communications and information flow that work for you

> Getting him and others involved/on board

> Helping make your success, their success, the team's success, their boss' success, and the organization's success – VERY IMPORTANT!

> Belief in yourself and what you are doing

Today I understand far better that there are almost always positive ways we can deal with difficult people and difficult situations. "No," doesn't really mean "NO!" if you can get someone interested and involved in what you are excited about. One of your most important tools in dealing with any difficult boss is setting the stage for your relationship to be as positive as possible. You do that by working with their shortcomings through a positive supportive approach while keeping in mind the importance of understanding their needs, wants, desires and intent and helping to fulfill those with judicious acknowledgement, appreciation, recognition, and respect.

When you set the stage the right way, you will have a better chance of putting on the play you want.

Vindictiveness

Sometimes it is very difficult to understand how you got on a person's bad side. If it is your boss, it can be very devastating to your work environment and your career. It is quite possible that it was something you said or did, or it certainly could have been something someone else said to your boss about you that caused this rift. It could be something that under normal circumstances and with a less paranoid, less sensitive, more ethical boss what happened or what was said would have meant nothing, but with your 'difficult' boss, you have hit a very sore nerve.

You do have recourses. They all go back to getting whatever this is about out in the open, even if your boss says she doesn't know what you are talking about. Then, begin to make amends.

Ask

> "Mary, we seem to have gotten off on the wrong foot and I know you are a great leader and quality person. I would like to know what I may have done wrong and what I can do to make amends. I really want to have a good, solid professional relationship with you and I want you to know I will support you at every turn."

Mary may respond in a variety of ways:

> If she tells you what is wrong, listen, thank her, assure her you are sorry and ask her how you can make amends.

> If she doesn't know, won't say, beats around the bush, make sure she knows that you are sincere about mending fences and that you are sincerely apologetic about having caused her any concerns.

You can also say something about rumor mills in general. And try to help her understand that if something has been said about you that you would like to clear the air and discuss the issue with her. Keep assuring her that your intentions are completely positive and supportive of her and what she is trying to accomplish.

This is only the start, but it is a necessary start. Regardless of how she responds, your next task is to follow-up with a supportive, positive, appreciative work attitude that she can't help but see. [See Chapters 9, 12-15]

> If you see any negativity from her in the future, jump on it right away with, "Ann, you seem upset with me, did I screw up? Is there anything I can do? I'm really sorry if..." and so on.

> Make sure at all times that she understands that you are open and honest and do not talk behind her back. Let her know that if you ever have any concerns, you will come directly to her. Sabotaging coworkers have often been the catalyst for a poor relationship with one's boss. Your aim is not to assign blame, but to make sure your boss knows who you are and how you do things.

Questions and Ideas for Contemplation

Hidden agendas and classic behind-your-back behaviors are not easy to root out, but it is possible if you find the most positive and open ways to deal with them. Be patient and stay open in spite of what else may happen. Some of your colleagues may have bought into your boss' way of doing things so your open and honest approach may need to be aimed in more than one direction.

The amazing thing is that it really is possible for these negative dynamics to change for the better through the efforts of one determined positive person. You can be that catalyst.

The predominant **intent** of passive-aggressive bosses:

Is often to 'get things done'

What they **need**: freedom from fear, which can be exacerbated by aggressive or passive-aggressive behaviors in others.

What they **want**: to be 'in control.'

What they **desire/care** about: being appreciated for who they are.

Chapter 23

POMPOUS BOSSES

Some bosses seem to need to be the center of attention, to hog the limelight. We see them as the ultimate egotists. While they can be outgoing and friendly, over time we begin to wonder if they really care about anyone except themselves.

How they operate

Pompous bosses tend to:

Be full of themselves

Dominate meetings, conversations, luncheon gatherings, etc.

Talk almost endlessly, often never quite focusing on the issues at hand

Have amusing (well at least they think so) stories and personal anecdotes that they share with everyone, typically time and time again

Not listen to others' ideas – or if someone manages to get a word or idea in edgewise, they are more than likely to completely ignore it in any consideration they make

Make decisions without considering anyone else's input

Not communicate why they change a group decision or recommendation, or give the reasons behind any given decision they make that goes against the grain of their employees' wishes

Be outgoing, friendly, everyone's buddy – but often in an obviously superficial way

The Result

This type of boss can be very demoralizing because team members feel overwhelmed by the 'presence' of this type of personality and also discover that their input, decisions, and efforts really don't make much of a difference. Everything is focused around this one person and what they want.

Basic Understanding

Pompous bosses have a very low self-image. Their need for the limelight and obsession with control, i.e. making important decisions against the wisdom of the evidence/data, is a cover-up for how they feel deep inside. They are 'Little Napoleons.'

Understanding this is critical to your success with them. Your first line of offense is to find ways to help fulfill their ego needs. (Hint: don't take a defensive stance with this type of boss; they will continue on their merry way.)

Most self-aggrandizing bosses actually do have a great deal of knowledge and competency. They may even be adequate, if not good, managers. Unfortunately, they let the 'ego-thing' take over when it comes to working with others. They make decisions based on how those decisions will reflect back on them. Their outgoing personality is something that should help them to be an effective leader. However, when coupled with their tremendous ego needs, this is where they tend to unfortunately fall flat.

Key Ideas

Appreciate, acknowledge who they are and what they are good at; do this daily in different ways. (See Chapters 8, 9, 12, and 13)

Help them make good decisions that are positive for them and the team. (See below, 'Tactics')

Acknowledge and Reward them for behaviors that are positive for the team, project, and/or individual. Hint: behavior modification when used in this type of positive way can be highly effective. Unfortunately, far too often, we forget how great this technique actually works and we don't use it.

NEVER use negative or neutral behavior modification techniques with this type of boss (i.e. ignoring them/looking away when they are on one of their many tangents in a meeting, then paying attention when they get on track). What they need is more attention. Probably more than we can give.

However, you can use other positive behavioral modification ideas in the same context. Give them extra attention and kudos when they get on track. SAY IT!

"Ralph, I really like your ideas on working through the manufacturing difficulties of the X widget. I think we can make a difference by incorporating them."

Keep it very simple when they stay on focus:

"That's great Ralph. We are really moving along with the issues here."

Help get other team members on this bandwagon. Bosses who need a lot of attention need A LOT of positive attention.

Tactics

The best skill you can develop with these over-the-top egotists is developing your ability to stay ahead of the game. If at all possible, don't give them the wiggle room to lose focus, make poor decisions, talk endlessly, or mis-communicate.

Focus

It can become very frustrating when you are scheduled for lengthy meetings with someone and you know that the end result will be that very little is covered, few important decisions are discussed or made, and no one else has much of a chance to give input, and when they do, it is almost assured to be ignored. After a while, everyone learns that two hours with so-and-so means two hours wasted.

What you can do

If you have any input into the organization of the meeting, you can make a major difference by getting everything important that needs to be covered, organized and down on paper. Even if you don't have specific input, give it anyway. List everything you want covered (BE BRIEF!) and get it out to everyone who will be at the meeting including the big cheese.

While he may not use your agenda, or will change it dramatically, and will probably get off track many times, at least you have set the stage with input that cannot be completely ignored because EVERYONE in the room also got it.

Often this type of preparation, done a day or two in advance, will generate a plethora of back and forth e-mails/memos. This helps get other team members involved. It also adds to the pie how much feedback your boss is getting about what is important for the upcoming meeting.

Brevity: Make any agenda very terse and focused. No explanations, suggestions, etc. You want this to be read. Almost all difficult bosses will ignore anything they can't digest in a few seconds. Make an outline list that highlights key points and possibly some essential sub-points, nothing else. Let any generated interest from other team members highlight discussion issues. [See Chapter 17, 'Information' for additional suggestions/examples for writing terse memos.]

During the meeting

Help keep things on tract. Be willing to stick your neck out a bit and help your boss maintain focus on important issues. This may be hard to do at first, but generally, used judiciously, this does not get pompous bosses upset.

> I was never very patient with managers who led meetings and consistently got off track. I learned very quickly that unless I wanted to waste a good bit of my valuable time, I needed to help push things along.

How to

When you have an opportunity to get a word in (not always easy), bring things back to focus. Be positive, and if feasible, find a way to be appreciative, or to acknowledge what your boss has done to this point.

> "Hal, that is great. Your comments on the x widget really help broaden our point of view. Now that we have this new perspective, I was wondering if we could look at the Kilroy data and try to make a decision about how we are going to get manufacturing up to speed.

Comment on the few things he did stay on track about.

Good idea: get as much specificity in as possible: data, considerations, etc. Get things on the table when you have the opportunity without taking a lot of time. Remember they want the limelight!

Raise your hand when you can't 'get in'

Unless the situation precludes it, i.e. this is NOT a good idea with your boss, raise your hand. It is the best means of letting a dominating talker know you have something to add. It may seem silly or out-of-place in a business meeting, but it works. [I have used this tactic dozens and dozens of times and never had anything negative come from it.]

Doing this does take some courage and a willingness to be assertive. If your boss really doesn't want you to do this, he/she will let you know. Then, back off from this tactic.

ASK!

When other means have failed, ask. A brief private meeting is the best venue for this discussion:

> "Ann, how would you like us to give you feedback or provide our perspectives when we are in a meeting. I feel a bit self-conscious about interrupting you when you are on a roll with a good idea, but sometimes what you say really gets me thinking and I want to jump off of your ideas."

Here you let her know what your needs are, while at the same time offering appreciation and support.

Helping them make GOOD Decisions

Sometimes pompous bosses seem to need to exert power and show control by making decisions, which on the surface seem to ignore the obvious wisdom of a group and the input of many people.

Open communications and information sharing are key tools you can use.

Get it down on paper

Key ideas need to be shared and they need to be obvious. BEFORE a key meeting, send an e-mail or memo to your boss detailing what you feel is most important. Keep it VERY terse. Something he/she can read in less than a minute. If you have more to add or say, do so in another e-mail to follow-up, perhaps later in the day. NEVER get on a soapbox and ramble on about merits, possibilities, etc. Your main purpose is to get things out in the open.

Send the memo to anyone and everyone who might be interested in the decision. This creates an obvious paper trail that becomes hard to ignore. It also gets others involved and on board.

Follow-up your memo with anyone who responds and send any follow-up ideas to your boss. The more these important ideas get out in the open, the better.

Help them be a part of good decisions

The more you can make these ideas, their ideas, the better. Couch things in terms of how their input, suggestions, etc. led to these considerations. Suggest that this will be exactly what their boss wants to see, and so on.

Making poor decisions better

You may hope for miracles, but don't expect them. Helping this type of boss get on track and stay on track may take a lot of time and energy. Sometimes you may have to make some hard decisions for yourself:

> Do you want to stay with this boss, division, organization?

> Are you unhappy enough to try to really make changes?

> Are you willing to stick your neck out to change things?

> Is all of this worth your effort?

If you can be as positive and as kind as possible when sticking your neck out to try to get something done or to change things, your boss may be willing to listen. If you are frustrated enough and you feel strongly enough to try to make changes, you should go ahead and make the effort.

A scenario

In spite of everything you and others have done (see above), your boss makes a decision for your team well outside your capabilities and your team's capabilities to follow-through with. You and fellow team members are upset because your input has been ignored. You feel like you have failed before you have even started on this project. Everyone is angry because your boss lowered the boom without any explanation or recourse for feedback.

Be willing to tell your boss what you think and how you feel. Set up a private meeting to discuss this important issue. Make this as professional as possible. Provide some kudos, appreciative statements, etc, but don't waste time. Get to the point.

> "Wayne, I was wondering if I could discuss this next quarter's goals with you. A lot of people down in manufacturing are pretty upset because we don't see any feasible way to meet the goals we just received. I know you want to push everyone

to be their best, and we are all willing to kick it into high gear for you every day, but over-realistic goals can be very demoralizing. I also worry about what Trish (Wayne's boss) will think if we don't even come close to making our quotas."

Important points

You are bringing the issue up by first by taking responsibility for your statements (using "I").

You are letting him know what the concern is in one sentence.

You are agreeing with your boss on motivations and perspective.

You are helping him focus on two key issues, both of which can be very influential with this type of boss: morale, and what their boss/higher ups may think as the result of this important decision.

Give them the opportunity to follow up without reacting defensively or negatively. You could get anything from, 'You are right," to "I will take this under consideration," to "I make the decisions around here and I don't care what you yahoos in manufacturing think. Don't waste my time whining. Get back to work."

You may not get positive results, but you have tried and that shows you respect yourself, your fellow workers, and that you have the chutzpah to be assertive when it counts. Your boss will notice. Unless he is a complete jerk, you will not have jeopardized anything. Plus, your boss will realize that he may be challenged on poor decisions he makes.

You do have to decide whether you want to take this step and stick up for what you think is right and best. If you get a worse- case scenario response, as in the latter one above, you might want to start looking for a new job, if you hadn't already. In other words, you may want to ask yourself if you really want to work for this type of boss any longer. Sometimes these harder choices may be the best one's for you and your family.

Poor communications

Earlier in this text we discussed many elements of good communications with difficult bosses. Here is a quick refresher relevant to communicating well with pompous bosses.

Open up communications at all levels

Someone has to start. It probably isn't going to be your difficult boss. The more you are open and forthright; the more others will feel free to jump on the bandwagon. Even if your boss doesn't buy into this right away, a very positive effect can be the interoffice dialogue you create, which will be hard for your boss to ignore completely over time.

Put EVERYTHING remotely important in writing

This helps open up communications

Keeps everyone involved and informed

Provides a paper trail

Keep communications positive and supportive

Important: reread every communiqué you send as if you were receiving it. Try to imagine how a person with poor self-esteem may interpret your approach/words.

Stay on track yourself

Terse, focused, professional communications are best. With a touch of positivity added, you can really make a difference with this type of boss.

Be willing to ask

If you haven't been informed, then make an effort to find out. You don't have any reason to complain if you haven't made an effort to find out from the horse's mouth.

It is wishful thinking that your difficult boss is going to open up without some effort on your part. When you make an effort, and keep up the positive information flow, he may very well begin to communicate more freely himself.

Someone needs to start the ball rolling, and while it may not seem fair, you are the one person who has the personal power, understanding, and compassion to make it happen in this important relationship in your work life.

The final analysis

You can be successful with pompous, self-aggrandizing bosses IF you take into account their egos and resulting eccentricities, AND if you use tactics and tools as suggested above to stay on top of problems.

Because these types of bosses can be pretty overwhelming, it is also critical to try to maintain your own self-worth without being overly defensive or aggressive. Let them be in their own space and find ways to keep on top of what is important to you.

Keep in mind that they are not likely to change personality in spite of your positive work with them. Your goal is to develop the skills to be successful with who they are and how they present to the world. As you develop better and better means of working with them, it is very likely they will learn better ways of working with you. Your self-confident willingness to act will make them take notice.

Questions and Ideas for Contemplation

The predominant **intent** of a pompous boss is

"to be cared for, to get along."

What they **need**: positive attention, kudos, appreciation, recognition, reward.

What they **want**: to be perceived as being in control, as being a nice person, as being 'Mr./Mrs. Wonderful.'

What they **desire/care** about: most importantly, how they appear to everyone, especially higher ups.

Chapter 24

INCOMPETENT BOSSES

Ideally, we hope that our boss will be a capable leader. Essentially, we expect him or her to be competent as to:

Expertise – knowledge, skills, and experience in a relevant area

Managing – ability to organize, delegate, allocate; in general, to run the nuts and bolts, every day responsibilities for their team

Leadership – motivate, inspire, mentor, and have the ability to create direction and energy for team members

Incompetent bosses typically lack skills in one or more of these areas.

How they got there

Luckily it is rare to find a boss who is completely devoid of all the qualities listed above. Many people in authority positions got there because:

They were experts in a field of knowledge, and were promoted because of their quality of work.

They had good managerial and organizational skills and were promoted to organize and run a team efficiently.

They were charismatic and worked well with others.

Another truth

People in authority positions, as we all do, have strengths and weaknesses.

A boss might be a great manager but have very poor people skills.

Another may know more than anyone else in the business about a specific area, but lacks any sense of how to keep a team together and running smoothly.

They might have a competent area of expertise relevant to a division of a business but lack a firm foundation in the entire scope of the area of the business they are now supervising.

They may have a tremendous energy and drive and are able to inspire talent and effort, but lack any sense of how to get things organized so the team can work efficiently.

And so on.

Appreciate, Acknowledge, and Use their Strengths

Know your boss (see Chapter 9). The better you understand what your boss does and doesn't bring to the table, the greater your success will be in working around, and with, their in-competencies.

When you can acknowledge that your boss does indeed have some areas of expertise, it is far easier to work with their deficiencies. It would be very unlikely to have a boss who lacks all skills and knowledge relevant to the business you are in, as well as in regards to managing and leadership.

Not too many people are placed in positions of authority JUST because they knew somebody, though it does happen. Plus, even if that were the case, everyone has strengths.

Find their strengths

By fully understanding your boss and his/her abilities, you will change your overall perception of who they are and what they are capable of. This effort can lead to the beginnings of respect for them as a person and authority figure.

They may still not come close to your perception of what a good boss should be, but you will have established a point from which you can both work together with, hopefully, mutual respect.

IMPORTANT: Respect is a key issue in working with someone and it has to start somewhere. If your boss does not show respect to other people, a BIG reason may be that he is not being shown respect in a way he recognizes or accepts. You can start the ball rolling by finding things that you CAN admire in him and start from there. His respect for you, your capabilities and potential, could jump off from there.

Acknowledge them for their strengths and, most importantly, let them know you **appreciate** these abilities. As always, it is important to SAY IT! E-mails, memos, passing comments, heart-to-heart talks – use whatever forums you can and use them often. A happy boss, a boss who feels appreciated, is more likely to be willing and able to work on their weaknesses if they feel good about themselves and their team.

> "Fred, I really admire your knowledge base in this area. I am encouraged to study more and work on my skills because of your example."

> "Tammy, you really have this office humming. I never thought we would get things organized after that last downsizing, but you have managed to get everyone in the right place and doing what they are good at. Kudos!"

> "Wayne, that was a great speech. I think everyone is on board to do their best on this next project. Thanks. I think we all needed that extra boost after so many changes last fall."

Use their strengths

When we appreciate someone for what they are good at, they will be sure to bring those abilities to the forefront of their work. You can further encourage them to use their strengths to benefit the team:

> "Jeanne, I need you to check through these figures for me. I know you have a keen eye, and I want to make sure everything is perfect before we send this further up the line."

> She may check it without your encouragement, but you have also gotten in a compliment. Plus – and this is important – it shows them you are also concerned with quality. This will help alleviate some of the tension right away between your boss, you, and others, relevant to her picking things apart **because** you are requesting it.

> "I was hoping you might give a little pep talk to the people in manufacturing today, Valerie. They are pretty down about losing Johnny, even though they know this move is best for his career. You have such a great way at helping people see the bright side of things. Thanks."

Support and Help them with their Weaknesses

If your boss is a complete disaster at organizing things and keeping things running smoothly, help them by taking up some of the mantle of responsibility in these key areas. It may be a bit of extra work, but it is going to make a major difference in your life at work and in how your team functions. Ultimately you will save time, headaches, and effort.

If your boss lacks good leadership skills, help him by taking on some responsibilities for mentoring colleagues, leading in times of change and crisis, motivating others when feasible, etc. Not only will work be a better place to be, but you will be gaining a great deal of experience, and very likely, appreciation in the process.

If your boss was brought in from another area to lead your team and has little specific understanding of what all of you are doing in the trenches, help educate him. Most people are eager to learn, if we don't put obstacles in their way, e.g. being disgruntled because this boss doesn't understand what is going on in manufacturing, having come from sales.

> I have worked with executive coaching clients in exactly this type of situation. Given the opportunity these managers made every effort to acquire as much understanding as possible about the new area they had been placed in to lead.

You may want to prioritize which 'boss deficits' you will want to help them with first if your boss has several. It is important to make sure you can handle the added responsibility that you may be assuming. You will probably find that in the long run your work life will be easier because you are not so frustrated.

We all want to be Good at what we do

When everything truly comes out in the wash, none of us want to be seen as incompetent. Unfortunately, egos, circumstances, personality conflicts, and other difficulties can get in the way and people end up disgruntled, angry, frustrated, etc. The most curmudgeonly of bosses would probably like to be seen as competent and, believe it or not, as likeable.

Support and encouragement can go a long way to making a less than ideal boss into someone much more willing to make an effort. It may take time. It will certainly take some time and work. It is worth it because this is YOUR work life.

Questions and Ideas for Contemplation

There are always ways to add positivity to the mix in any difficult situation. After making an effort to understand your difficult boss' strengths and weaknesses, can you envision ways in

157

which you and your colleagues can make a difference by your willingness to encourage, support, and appreciate your boss?

Try different approaches and strategies. See what works best. Be judicious. There are many key ideas throughout this text that can help. Always start from a position of strength by having set the stage through encouragement, support, and respect for the competencies they do possess.

Chapter 25

PASSIVE BEHAVIORS

Some bosses can be frustrating and obstructionist because of <u>what they don't do</u>. You are ready to charge the halls of Montezuma with a great idea or new approach, but they can't seem to get their act together to make any kind of decision. You might not hear from them for extended periods of time and no matter what you try, you can't seem to get any response from them.

> I once worked in an organization where one of the senior bosses never responded to any communiqué unless he wanted to. Memos, e-mails, projects, papers, potential contracts, etc,, all essentially were forgotten and discarded unless this high level authority figure had it in mind to respond. After a while, you simply learned that if you hadn't heard from him, your idea or project was 'dead.'

Uncommunicative, waffling, unreliable, inept, unavailable bosses can be VERY frustrating to work with, and in some ways even more difficult, because it is tough to get enough information to understand them. Understanding this type of boss can be as difficult as trying to get something done with them.

Fear is the likely culprit

Their approach to life is quietly defensive. 'If I don't rock the boat, we won't get swamped.' And they translate this passive resistance to include pretty much anyone on their team. 'You better not rock the boat either.'

How did they get into positions of leadership?

> They didn't rock the boat.

Help them Feel Safe

The best tactic you can take with this type of difficult boss is to help them to feel safe in your presence, with your abilities, and with making decisions. Different bosses will react to different techniques; however, there is often a good bit you can do.

Safety First

Avoid all signs of negativity: as frustrated as you may feel, you can't let them know. Keep facial expressions and gestures neutral or positive. Getting upset will more than likely send them deeper into hiding.

Use clear, positive communications that are direct and simple to understand and respond to. Anything complicated can be misinterpreted and can create further impasse.

Be willing to ask — not only to ask, but to ask very specifically for the information you need, the decisions that need to be made, etc. Generalities are safer than being locked into something, so indecisive and reluctant managers like to hide behind them.

Support and encourage open communications and decision making. The more positive you can be the better. **Reinforce the behaviors you want to see!** Gently and calmly suggest, cajole, offer assistance, do whatever it takes to open up the communications with your reluctant boss. When they do respond, make decisions, etc. reinforce that behavior with positive encouragement.

Be willing to take on responsibility for making decisions, taking on tasks, etc. Reluctant bosses often leave us windows of opportunity so we can get things done ourselves, and where we can learn and develop our own expertise and authority.

Make decisions; take responsibility — just make sure you let them know what you are doing.

> E-mail: "Karla, I'm going to move ahead with the Jones contract and send it up the line this afternoon unless you have any further input. Thanks for letting me work on this. I think we have a great chance for success and the VP should be pleased with what you and I have put together." [Always kick in the positive whenever you have the opportunity. This is a wise way to encourage further decision-making and effort on her part even if she really didn't contribute much to this project.]

Your Ego

It can be tough to give up our complete ownership of our work to help our boss — who we really feel doesn't deserve any recognition for our efforts. When that little voice inside starts to fight back and resist, you know your ego is in play.

Can you give up a bit of ego and ownership for more peace of mind?

Remember that self-worth, self-confidence, and self-control work much better in difficult situations with difficult people, and your kindness and compassion mean far more to you and others, than giving up some ego.

Be Clear and Specific

Make sure they understand what you want: be very specific and clear about the decisions you need them to make, what you need them to do, what you plan to do, etc. Put it in writing at every opportunity. Make the decisions as easy as possible for them to make. If you have all your ducks in a row, then, while their input may be minimal, at least they can feel like they can make a safe decision. It may set the stage for better involvement from them in the future, or at the very least more freedom for you to act.

Be very patient. Offer to assist in any way you can, but ultimately you need to give them the space to make some decisions and get things done, too. Badgering your boss will likely create ill will and more reluctance to act in any constructive way.

Make sure you clarify your responsibilities, authority, and work load. You can do this even if your boss is reluctant to specify anything. Write down what you believe your work responsibilities and authority are and send this memo to your boss and team members for responses. You will then have opened the topic up to everyone and will have documentation of what you feel are your duties. (Bramson)

When helping your boss with any of his responsibilities, workload, decision-making, etc. make sure you keep documentation of what you are doing and why.

Acknowledge, appreciate, and recognize them when opportunities are present to do so. Find ways to create opportunities by making it easy for them to succeed. Get your coworkers on board the same program. The more positivity and encouragement, the more likely your boss will come out of his shell.

Help them to feel part of the team. 'Reluctant to be involved' bosses often feel left out. Though their behavior seems to warrant even less involvement, their basic intent is 'to get along.' Help them to become an active and involved member of the team.

When in doubt, put it in writing. Writing something down helps clarify things that we need to understand better, and when we send it to others it essentially says a number of things:

This is important enough for me to put it on paper.

There is now a record of this idea, decision, effort, etc.

I am doing such and such about this or that.

Other people have been informed of what I am up to

A lot of extra work?

You may be thinking that you already have too much to do without having to nursemaid your boss. The real truth in working successfully with relationships of all kinds is that our efforts, while they may take a little extra time initially, pay us back in many ways in the long run. When our frustration levels decrease, so does all of that wasted energy, (not to mention the time we used up beating our heads against the wall).

Being proactive in working with this type of boss can pay major dividends. Not only can you end up helping them and helping your team, but you will probably find that you have learned a great deal, taken on more responsibility, and developed some admirable leadership qualities. All of which can help, if you plan to further your career.

Questions and Ideas for Contemplation

There are thousands of scenarios that could be envisioned where an authority figure's passivity causes a great deal of discomfort and stress in an organization. The ideas above can be tailored to the individual situation you find yourself in, if you are willing to take the time to consider the nature of your boss' reluctance to act, and if you are patient in trying a variety of skills and techniques to help them move ahead.

The predominant **intent** of passive bosses:

Avoid conflict; feel safe.

What they **need**: freedom from fear which can be exacerbated by aggressive or passive-aggressive behaviors in others.

What they **want**: to be 'in control' without any trauma or conflict

What they **desire/care** about: being appreciated for who they are, getting along, being a part of the team

When in doubt about how to approach a difficult authority figure, you can always return to *The Seven Keys to Understanding and Working with Difficult People*; consider these in the context of your proposed actions and to see if what you plan to say and do fits:

Self-Awareness

Are you **aware** of how you will come across to this person and how their eccentricities will impact your ability to deal successfully with them? Can you stay on top of your feelings, thoughts, and reactions as you work with them?

Self-Worth

Are you feeling **good about yourself**?

Are you bringing your best YOU to the fore?

Self-Confidence

Are you **confident** in your strategy and in your ability to do what you want to do?

Self-Control

Can you maintain **control** of your reactions in spite of what they do or say (or don't do and don't say)? Positivity breeds Positivity.

Honesty

Can you be open and **honest** about your motives and actions?

Kindness

Can you find ways to be **kind** (and compassionate) in dealing with this person's concerns?

Positivity

Can you maintain your **positivity** in spite of the difficulties of this situation and the concerns you have with this person?

Chapter 26

NEGATIVITY

"Negativity breeds Negativity"

The overall aura of an office can be affected in many ways and unfortunately negativity can pervade an organization or team very rapidly. Sometimes it is difficult to identify what caused this doom and gloom atmosphere, though we often like to have someone or something to blame:

Them

The organization/culture/management in general

A specific event or series of events

Circumstances

The business climate

Your boss and/or his boss

A colleague or clique of colleagues

Perceptions are everything

How we and others perceive our work and the climate in which we work makes a huge difference in whether we are able to enjoy what we do, and whether we feel we have the freedom to do it in the way we think we should. It is very important to keep in mind that everyone's perceptions are different. While we may all share a dislike for a person's approach to us or their demeanor, or for the general atmosphere in an office, the truth is we all interpret these things somewhat differently. It is also quite common that one person's perception of a negative event may be diametrically opposite of another person.

For example: It would not be usual for a somewhat paranoid, depressed, insecure boss to see your successful completion of a project and the resultant kudos you receive as not only a challenge to their success and well-being, but quite possibly as a catastrophic problem.

Whether consciously or subconsciously, they feel a need to deal with this problem. Their approach to dealing with it may be to: put you down; find ways to sabotage your further success; blame, complain, whine; etc.

> Author's Note: I had a boss who would find something to get me on or complain about anytime I had any type of success. It got to the point where I could predict when he would show up the day after something I had accomplished. I really don't think he had any idea he was doing it. It was very frustrating, because I never got the appreciation from him that I felt I deserved. Though I recognized this eccentricity in him and was able to deal with it on one level, eventually I felt compelled to move on.

Most importantly

To reiterate a point made several times already:

Difficult people very often do not see themselves as difficult.

This is likely true even if your fellow team members also see your boss as being very difficult.

Blaming, complaining, whining, rude, boorish, NEGATIVE people rarely see themselves as being so pervasively negative.

Also, very important

It isn't your task and it shouldn't be one of your goals to point out another person's negativity – particularly your boss'! Negativity will breed negativity. There are better choices.

Are you adding to the mix?

If you have been unhappy at work, i.e., frustrated, upset, depressed, etc., it is quite likely that you have been adding to the overall negative feeling that may be pervading your work life. It takes a willingness to spend some serious soul searching and self-observation to truly understand how we are impacting others.

From long experience, both personal and through work with clients, being aware of and taking responsibility for what we say and do and how we say and do it is hard work. If we take the time to do this work, we will learn a great deal about ourselves and we will be able to make a major difference in how we approach work, our colleagues, and our boss. We will also understand much better how we add to the mix, either negatively or positively.

We need to be willing to face our own negativity and take responsibility for it – disparaging self-talk affects us in our daily interactions with others. Through self-observation we can begin to turn our inner negativity around, so that the face we present to the world continues to be more and more positive.

Ask yourself and pay attention every day:

Do you blame others?

or

Do you take responsibility for your life and work?

Do you complain?

or

Do you try to seek solutions to problems and concerns?

Do you whine?

or

Are you proactive about changing things for the better?

Are you depressed?

or

Do you find ways to take care of yourself and others?

Negativity   or   **Positivity**?

Choose wisely

Who are YOU to THEM?

Do you really know how you come across to others? Have you asked anyone?

Many times, what we think of as a normal, business appropriate, professional approach, may be perceived as negative by someone else. This is particularly true of someone who has lived with negativity a long time and is very sensitive to any hint of criticism.

> For example: if you tend to approach things professionally, pedantically, with an eye for insisting on detail and high quality, a creative/sensitive person might find your approach brusque, even rude or demeaning.

Through careful observation we can come to understand how what we do and say impacts others – if you are brave, it doesn't hurt to ask, either.

When we know how we impact others. We can make a positive difference, in our life and in theirs.

By being open and honest with ourselves and by sharing that understanding with others, fellow team members, our boss, and our employees, we can go a long way toward mitigating these types of difficulties/negativity. Let them know who you are and how you approach things at work:

> "Mike, I know I sometimes come across somewhat demandingly. Please understand that it is my desire to get things right and to have the whole team be their best that drives this. It isn't personal. I really don't mean to pick on you. I will certainly try to do better. If I seem to come down on you too hard at some point, please excuse my inherent nature to push ahead. I admire your work and know you are always trying to do your best. By the way, if I get a bit rough around the edges, feel free to let me know. It helps me to do better and it will help me to understand the types of things that I do that are of concern to you and others."

We can always learn more about ourselves. Sharing who we are with others helps us open up doors to further understanding of them and of ourselves. Most people will appreciate your candor and will respond more positively because they will understand you better.

Negative Bosses

As the head of a team, group, or organization bosses have tremendous influence over the overall tenor and dynamics of the people within their purview. A boss who tends to spread doom and gloom, who complains and whines, blames others, is rude and brusque with people, treats people badly, lies, backstabs, etc., can infect an entire team or organization. Not only can they spread their negativity like a disease, it is very common for some of their employees to buy into their approach and their way of doing things, making the whole situation more stressful and depressive.

It is also important to realize that all types of difficult bosses (the difficult behaviors that they use) create negativity within a team. We can choose to work from two perspectives:

How can I work to change the overall aura of this office?

How can I work to be successful with my boss' difficult behaviors?

There is hope

Most of us are not over-the-top enthusiastic, bubbly personalities. While having this type of personality might be useful, a generally positive approach to everyone in **your purview** at work can make a significant difference over time to the overall atmosphere in which you all work.

Uncomfortable?

It is common when we decide to initiate this type of approach that we feel somewhat ill at ease.

First of all, you may be bucking the whole general atmosphere and approach by everyone else in the office.

Secondly, this very well may not be 'you' and it does take time for us to feel comfortable with a new approach.

Start slowly

Start by giving a few compliments, a 'thank you,' a small gift or reward, and so on for work well done. Spread this around. If your major aim is to have a better and more comfortable place in which to work, and to be successful in your work, you will make the most impact if you work this magic with everyone.

While your boss may be the major contributor to the office's overall negativity, you will be more comfortable, and seen in a better light by everyone, if you spread the good feelings around. This helps eliminate any thoughts and feelings by others that you are trying to get on your boss' good side, or that you might be seen as a bootlicker.

Note: Many great ideas for spreading positivity throughout an office have already been given in this book (see Chapters 9, 11, and 13).

Every time you support someone, acknowledge and appreciate them, recognize them for who they are and what they do, you are helping create a different, more positive atmosphere in the face of whatever negativity abounds. Keep at it and some people will join you. You may get a few converts right away; others could take considerably longer to come around. Stay the course. It is worth it!

Add Humor, Add Joy

Gentle, good-natured humor can help. Even somewhat goofier humor has its place, depending on how you feel it would fit in. The more relaxed the atmosphere, and the more relaxed you can make it, the more fun and joy that can be generated over time.

The Truth

Most people would far prefer to have a positive working environment than not, and they will notice, at least subconsciously, that something in the office has changed. Some, and then a few more, will begin to add positivity also. Many people will respond to kindness with kindness, support with support, and appreciation for who they are and what they do with an appreciation for who you are and what you do...

Kindness breeds Kindness

Respect breeds Respect

Appreciation breeds Appreciation

Recognition breeds Recognition

And so on.

It has to start somewhere. **Why not with you?**

Choose wisely.

Stick to your guns

Change takes time. Negativity, especially long-inbred and pervasive negativity, takes time to change. We all have our 'up' days and our 'down' days. When you just don't feel on top of things, take care of yourself (see Chapter 11), and try to make what effort you can for that moment in time.

169

Seeking others' support and help when you have personal concerns can also be very important to eventually changing overall office dynamics for the better. Don't be afraid to talk to other team members and get them on board. Be willing to ask for help and support. Be willing to talk about what you are trying to do with those team members you feel you can trust.

You will feel better and be more effective if you have support.

People like to help.

People like to feel needed.

It feels good to help each other.

Changing the overall dynamics of an office and group can take a long time – weeks, months, a year or longer. Be patient and keep spreading positivity. If you really want to notice changes that occur, take some notes at various stages. This will help give you some reference points and a better perspective of what you are about as well:

Week one: Started my positivity campaign today. Gave three compliments and thanked half a dozen people for their efforts. Several people seemed genuinely embarrassed by what I said and most really seemed surprised....

Week three: I actually got two compliments when I walked into the office today – one from the boss' administrative assistant (with a big smile) and one from Elmer who has been working with me closely on this latest project. Elmer was a big surprise. He is usually pretty reserved and was often kind of morose and down-in-the-dumps. I always thought Beth was a nice person, but she has been treated so badly by David, I really worried about her....

Don't try to change your boss

It is certainly tempting to go in and tell your boss you think he is rude, abrasive, depressive, and a negative influence, but it is not going to change him, and it certainly isn't going to help you. Positivity work aims at change through mostly subtle means. If you stick to your guns and work hard at this with others on your team and with your boss in as positive way as possible, you will make a difference with everyone. It would be the rare, extremely difficult boss, that wouldn't be affected by this over the long haul.

Remember that your best ammunition for working positive 'magic' with your boss is to understand him (i.e. know her needs, wants, desires, and intent). The better you understand what is driving her, the better you can tailor your approach. [See also Chapter 9, "Knowing Your Boss"]

If your boss is an inveterate complainer...

> Be solution oriented.

If your boss spreads doom and gloom...

> Be positive and upbeat with them no matter what they say. See the silver-lining to their dark clouds.

If your boss is a blamer and doesn't take responsibility for things...

> Don't blame and complain. Take responsibility, be positive, say good things about people, show them there are other ways to look at things (don't point your finger at them either).

Choose positivity in the face of negativity

Though change may be slow in coming, and you probably won't change their overall approach to the world, you WILL make a difference, and you will feel better for your own choices, regardless of the choices your boss makes. [My clients are proof positive that this works!]

All those little things

It is the little daily efforts you make that will have the most profound effect over time.

Start today!

Questions and Ideas for Contemplation

A self-analysis is a good place to start on a quest for spreading more positivity.

You can also do a thorough analysis of the people and the office dynamics that seem to add to the general negativity at work. Ask these questions:

Who is adding to the negativity pool? How? (Be specific.)

How is our boss affecting the overall office dynamics? What is he doing that seems to affect me/us so negatively? (Be very specific.)

What interpersonal dynamics (cliques, etc.) add to the concerns and how?

When you accomplish this, you will have a better understanding of what is affecting your work environment and have a feel for the best skills and tactics to use and with whom. Hint: Do this on paper or on the computer; it will be easier to put it all into perspective. Be sure to keep this and any sensitive information from prying eyes.

Though it seems their approach is designed to accomplish just the opposite, negative people want to feel accepted, acknowledged, and appreciated.

Everyone appreciates being understood and acknowledged.

If you want to be helpful and proactive, go with the idea that you want to help this person and to make the best of a difficult situation for yourself, your team, and your business.

Chapter 27

SERIOUS NEEDS AND CONCERNS

Bosses with Serious problems

There are bosses with serious physical, behavioral, and emotional problems. Luckily, they are very few in number. If all that you have tried has failed, and you absolutely feel this situation is beyond your control, then it is wise to get help.

By all means you should use your best knowledge, skills, and tools to make a difference with this person. Many of the ideas presented in this book may prove helpful even if you are dealing with a person with serious personal problems. However, you have to be the final judge as to whether you can be successful with this person or whether you need to get help.

A little knowledge CAN be a dangerous thing

Please DO NOT attempt to diagnose a person's condition yourself. Unless you are a qualified psychologist, psychiatrist, social worker, counselor, or physician and have specific professional diagnostic training you should NEVER label someone with a mental or emotional disorder or physical condition or illness. There are ample venues at most places of business where you can report your concerns and allow professionals to deal with them.

While you may gather evidence (see below) of what you feel are serious concerns relative to your boss' behavior(s), keep in mind that because this is personally impacting you, it is very difficult to maintain an unbiased perspective of what you are witnessing. Your best course of action is to involve appropriate professionals from your business community and/or get personal help for yourself: coach, mentor, counselor, legal help, Human Resources, etc.

GET HELP!

Never put yourself or anyone else at serious risk.

Being kind, open, compassionate, and understanding are positive ways to deal with difficult bosses and a great way to approach everyone in general; however, sometimes we have to make safe decisions if the situation has not improved or has gotten worse. You can always continue your positive approach while seeking help with serious concerns.

Things to look for

Aberrant or strange behavior

Extreme behavior

      Frequent uncontrolled outbursts

      Marked change in behavior

      Significant fluctuations in mood

Threats

Physical symptoms

Noticeable alcohol or drug usage

What to do

I always advocate using the ideas presented in this book as a first step in dealing with difficult people. There usually are many things that you can do to effect change by working with the ideas presented in *The Seven Keys to Understanding and Working with Difficult People,* and by trying the wide variety of techniques, skills and tools recommended in this book. However, there are times when we have to draw a line and make other choices. Choices that, while they may be difficult for us to make, in the long run will be safer and wiser for all concerned:

      Get help

          From your organization

          From without

      Change positions within an organization

      Get a new job

Getting Help

Document what you are concerned about. Be very specific and list occurrences, dates and times, who may have been present, exactly what you observed, what they did and said, how you reacted, as well as what you did and said, etc. Be as detailed as possible. Keep in mind your emotions may color your perceptions, so the more specific you are the better. This kind of log can also help you take a step back and observe your concerns from a slightly detached perspective after the experience or event. You will gain better insight over time of the entire situation.

If you feel it is important or necessary, **report your concerns** to an appropriate venue at work or an authority figure. Present them with information in such a way that 1) you show you are concerned for the person involved and are willing to help work toward a solution – this can help make them take you more seriously, and 2) you feel that this concern may be serious enough that it is beyond your knowledge and skills to deal with.

Let them know that you have documented your concerns.

Follow-up. If the situation is this troubling, you should make sure there is some follow through. Though one would hope this would not be the case, some managers and Human Resource departments may try to ignore your concerns, because it is easier than admitting a problem. You have to be willing to continue to pursue a serious concern because it is your life and work, as well as the lives and work of anyone this person interacts with, that are at risk.

Get help personally. This can be a tough time. Make sure you have support from friends and relatives, and if needed, professionally from a coach, counselor, minister, or mentor.

Get help legally if you feel this is necessary for your own protection. This may be a resource you will need to pursue if your place of work refuses to take action on your concerns.

This can be Difficult

These types of difficult situations require a great deal of fortitude. You may have to work through a very stressful period while this issue is addressed. Make the best choices you can for yourself and for your loved ones and be willing to make hard choices when you need to.

Be sure to take care of yourself. Pay particular attention to how you are holding up and how your family/loved ones are weathering this, too. What is affecting you WILL affect others.

Get out?

In spite of everything you have tried there are situations in life where we feel as if we are caught between a rock and a hard place. We still, always, have choices we can make. Sometimes they are very difficult choices. If your whole life and enjoyment of life is at stake, then the wisest choice may be to find a different position.

> Author's note: As I look back on the many decisions I have made over my lifetime, even the really difficult ones that required giving up something significant to move ahead, I have always found that in the long run these decisions were for the best.

When you have to make a hard decision, choose to make the most of your life and work. Choose for your family and for yourself.

Questions and Ideas for Contemplation

It is very tempting to categorize people into neat 'types' so that we can explain their eccentricities and give ourselves an out. It is much harder to take responsibility for ourselves and for our actions and words when we are involved with a very difficult person or situation and to make choices that are best and wisest for everyone concerned.

Your boss, difficult, ornery, 'crazy,' paranoid, or…is a human being, no less than you and I. Kindness and consideration should always be part of the equation when you are working with others. Though we may find that over the long haul we can't work or be successful with this person, we can still be compassionate. It keeps us human. It keeps us alive.

Chapter 28

REALLY DIFFICULT BOSSES

Yes, there are bosses who seem to be almost impossible to deal with successfully. Their behaviors are so far over-the-top that it is difficult to even know where to start. If you have a boss who is 'over-the-top-difficult,' you could probably take the list of difficult behaviors at the end of Chapter 19 and find that a good many of them apply to your boss.

This is actually a great exercise to go through as it gives you a needed perspective on the behaviors that are frustrating and upsetting to you and others. By delineating behaviors and concerns, you set the stage for how you can approach these specific issues, which is much easier than dealing with someone who is 'really difficult.'

Remember: even really difficult bosses may not have a clue of how they impact others.

Can you be successful with them?

Very likely, yes. However, there are a few caveats.

You always have choices you can make:

To live with the problem and try to be the most positive best person you can be in spite of who your boss is and what he does

To try the ideas and recommendations in this book for a significant period of time and see if they make a difference. Remember any form of negativity can erase any positive work that went before. You have to make a sincere commitment to positive, constructive work for an extended period of time.

To get help: coach, counselor, Human Resources or other agency at work, or another administrator

To seek a different situation – in the same organization or elsewhere

To get legal assistance or guidance

Safety first – don't put yourself or anyone else in jeopardy; get out if you need to

> Serious concerns – your boss may have a serious physical, mental, or emotional problem (see Chapter 27). He/she may need help. While it may not be smart to jump the gun and blame him/her for something you suspect, it is wise to play it safe and get help if you feel this is beyond your ability to deal with.

How to be successful?

You have already started by reading this book and developing an understanding of the skills, tools, and techniques that can be successful with difficult bosses. By making a sincere effort to develop and use this knowledge, you can make a difference. It is certainly possible that you could make a _major_ difference in how your boss interacts with you, and even in your whole work situation.

Important: Keep in mind that the object is not to change your boss. Rarely will we be successful, if we direct our efforts at changing someone else.

What we aim at is changing the dynamics of our relationship

with another person so they treat us

the way we want to be treated.

This is not only possible, but often quite feasible. While there is always some chance that our positive actions may effect permanent change in another person, far too often their personalities and behavior patterns are much too ingrained; unless, of course, they decide to take up the mantel of change for themselves.

Change yourself, make positive life-affirming changes, and you WILL change the world you live and work in.

Difficult bosses on the edge

Some, even many, people who are having difficulties with life are over-worked, stressed, anxious, and beat-up. A compassionate, positive approach may indeed work wonders with them. If you and others are not in any immediate danger, it is probably worth a try. Very often a dose of kindness, a willingness to be open and honest, and an effort to be supportive and understanding can make all the difference in the world to a person who is on the edge.

Sometimes all it takes is paying some attention to their concerns, paying attention to them, and by being appreciative of who they are, especially their strengths.

The ideas and techniques in this book do work. Yes, this can take time and a good bit of perseverance. There may be set-backs. Stick with it and I truly believe that in the vast majority of circumstances you will make a difference with even the most curmudgeonly of bosses. Plus, you will feel good about what you are trying to do. And, you will very likely become a positive influence throughout your work place, which can also have a positive effect on all your interactions at work and on your career.

'On purpose' bosses

There are a few bosses who actually seem to behave in certain ways on purpose.

> They see aggressive behavior as a way to get things done.

> They see themselves, what they do, and what they believe as better than someone or something else and more righteous than other people. They may even feel it is their 'divine right' to act as they do, e.g., Phariseeism. (Meier)

> They don't ever see themselves as responsible or guilty.

> They seem to lack a conscience, lack remorse, and/or feel no empathy for others.

> They may be excessively paranoid and think you (and the rest of the world) are out to get them.

> They may be highly unethical, but feel no concern about what they do that impacts others negatively. (Hoover)

It is certainly possible that given a qualified analysis, some of these individuals might be diagnosed with a borderline mental or emotional condition/disorder as described in the *Diagnostic and Statistical Manual of Mental Disorders* (*DSM-IV*) of the American Psychiatric Association, but that is something for highly qualified professionals to determine. Your responsibility is to make the best possible decisions you can make for yourself and for those close to you.

A boss who uses his position and power to consistently demean, force others to his/her will, purposely hurts others, or who doesn't care about others, has no reason to be in a position of authority. He may be a power figure, but he is not a leader. You can make an effort to work with this kind of person or you can choose to find a better situation for yourself. It is well worth your while to try the ideas presented in this book, but if things do not get better, your best options are to get help and to find a better professional situation for yourself.

Get help

Support and encouragement from friends, relatives, colleagues you trust

Counseling

Professional Coaching/Mentor: executive and personal coaches are trained to help you through difficult situations and concerns. [At difficultpeople.org and Metacoach LLC we train our coaches specifically in the areas of helping clients with difficult people concerns and difficult situations at work.]

Legal guidance, if you feel you need this type of support and security

Make positive choices for yourself even if it means making

a major change at work and in your life

If you have made a sincere effort to get along, do your work professionally, and worked with understanding and positivity, I can think of very few reasons to stick around with a boss who has serious problems. Your life, well-being, and enjoyment are at risk. Your family's life, well-being, and enjoyment are also probably at risk. Make a difference today for yourself and your loved ones by seeking a better solution. We always have choices; sometimes they are tough to make.

Questions and Ideas for Contemplation

Consulting another person, close friend, relative or colleague, is an initial way you can begin to understand and make a difference in being successful with a really difficult boss. Simply talking things out and trying to understand the dynamics of a given situation can help. Periodic sharing of your experiences, efforts, successes and set-backs, can help you keep a good perspective on things and can give you a jumping off point for what you decide to do next.

Avoid blaming and other forms of negative thinking.

Try to focus on understanding and finding solutions.

A personal and executive coach can also provide an excellent outside perspective and he/she will offer you support, encouragement, understanding, and suggestions to help you be successful. Though this can be a significant investment in money, you will find that it can be extremely helpful and worthwhile. A coach can give you a whole new perspective on your concerns and help you find many different means for achieving your desires and goals.

Chapter 29

HARASSING BEHAVIOR

Harassment, Discrimination, and Prejudicial Behaviors

You should never tolerate behaviors that are inappropriate.

Harassment can come in a variety of forms. If you are uncomfortable with behavior that seems inappropriate, discriminatory, harassing, or prejudiced there are things you can do. In this chapter we will examine a series of steps that work well with approaching these types of concerns.

> Note: many companies address these issues in their employee handbooks or other documentation. Use these as a reference point for further understanding and action. Regulations may dictate how you should respond to inappropriate behaviors/actions of your boss. It is important to read these documents thoroughly and to take appropriate action. Fundamentally, how you approach these concerns will be your decision.

Sexual Harassment

Essentially the legal description for sexually inappropriate behavior is whether *a reasonable woman or man would find the behavior to be sexual harassment. Obviously, this leaves some questions about exactly how this might be interpreted by our legal system.

What is most important is how the behavior affects you. If YOU feel that a behavior is inappropriate or offensive, it is probably worth taking initial steps to curtail it or deal with it by bringing your concerns forward to the person(s) perpetrating the behavior, an agency at work, or another authority figure. [See Note above about company regulations.]

Discrimination

Discrimination is treating someone differently because of some characteristic or trait.

For example:

Race or ethnicity

Creed or religion

On the basis of gender

Handicapped individuals

Specific laws cover these issues and appropriate authorities, human resources departments, and government sources can provide current information. NOTE: If at some point you feel the need to pursue your concern legally, please contact an appropriate agency and/or get a lawyer qualified in this area.

Prejudicial behavior

Prejudices can be very concerning. Unfortunately, they are often legally, ethically, and practically very hard to define and pin-down. Well-documented concerns, however, can and should be addressed if they are causing significant problems and discomfort at work. It is not unusual for people to have minor (and even major) prejudices of which they are unaware. Drawing attention to your concern with the perpetrator may be all that is necessary for the behavior to cease.

Dealing with inappropriate, harassing, discriminatory, and prejudicial behaviors

Putting up with these types of behaviors, particularly over the long haul, can be very demeaning and devastating. You have the right and you should make an effort to do something to alleviate the concern. Please note: you always have the choice of getting professional support from within your business (Human Resources or other appropriate venue) and legal advice, if you feel you need further guidance.

Know your Organization's policies

If you have concerns about any type of inappropriate behavior, you should read through the policies published by your business very carefully. If you do not know where to find them, check with Human Resources. It is very important to know how these issues are expected to be handled and what options you have when you feel that your concerns have reached a point where you want and/or need support and assistance. If you have any doubts as to the proper procedures, the meaning of a guideline or policy, or what you should do next, contact a Human Resources professional and sit down and discuss your options.

Carefully Document the issues and concerns you have

Even if the documentation is only your word against theirs, the fact that you have gone to the trouble to keep detailed records gives your complaint more legitimacy. Be honest and professional, regardless of the other person's behavior/approach to you. In any type of complaint, documentation is VERY important.

Keep detailed notes of every instance:

> The specific behavior, verbiage, actions, facial expressions, gestures, and tone of voice of the perpetrator

> Date and sign each entry

> Keep an extra copy in a safe place – a safety deposit box is ideal. DO NOT allow access to this information to anyone unless you absolutely trust them. It is probably NOT a good idea to have this type of information stored on an office computer.

> Share this information with a trusted relative or friend.

Discussing your concerns with a trusted person helps you document the whole process and can provide you tremendous support. DO NOT keep these types of concerns to yourself. It is very important to let someone else know what you are concerned about and why. Be willing to be open and specific, even if the whole situation is embarrassing and awkward at first.

If anyone has been a witness to any of these incidents, ask them if they would be willing to witness your account. Whether they do or not, note their presence.

You can note/document their response to your request. They may offer valuable information. Be specific.

> When I asked Barbara to witness Mike's sexual innuendos, she got very pale and frightened: "I really want to help you out, Ann, but I'm scared of Mike. He threatened to fire me when I asked him to stop. Just be quiet and put up with it. He has done a lot worse to some other women. Remember when Elsie quit? Keep quiet and be careful about this because he thinks he owns everyone in this office." She seemed genuinely scared and has avoided talking with me since this incident.

If there is another person at work who shares these same concerns, talk to them about what you are doing and ask them if they would like to keep their own records and/or work with you on resolving this joint issue. You can document your conversation with them whether they are willing to help back you up or not.

Bring it out in the open

At some point after you have documented several incidents you should bring your concerns to the attention of someone at work or directly to the perpetrator.

IMPORTANT: I have found that the following steps, taken in order, work extremely well. This is a personal decision and you must decide how to proceed with your own situation/case. One option is to decide whether to take this issue to an appropriate agency at your place of work, hire legal assistance, request mediation, etc. Make sure you are comfortable with the decision you make to go forward. Only you can make this decision. Err on the side of caution and get assistance if you have any doubts. Requesting mediation is an excellent choice at this juncture.

At your initial meeting

Set this up as a formal, sit-down, secure meeting with the perpetrator. Close the door when you arrive. You want this to be professional and you want your boss to take what you have to say seriously.

Try to be/stay calm and professional

Use non-accusatory language – own what you say

> "John, I am concerned about one issue between us that I would like to bring up. I know you may not mean this in any negative way, but I feel very uncomfortable when you address me as 'Honey,' 'Sweetie,' 'Babe,' and so on. I also feel you have made some suggestive comments when we have been alone and this also makes me very uncomfortable. Could we talk about this and come to some agreement as to what we both feel is appropriate?"

Your boss may not have a clue that what he is doing is making you uncomfortable. And unless he has been living with his head in the sand for the past twenty plus years, he will get the point immediately. He may, very likely, be embarrassed, apologize immediately, and promise to watch what he says in the future.

Document any meetings that take place relative to this issue.

If the behavior does not improve or if there are further concerns, take the next step -- a second meeting or take this to Human Resources. Be sure to continue your documentation.

Second meeting

> NOTE: Consideration for a second meeting is an entirely personal decision. Many people feel that one meeting/warning is enough and if the behavior doesn't change, you should immediately get professional assistance in pursuing the matter further. Other people are more comfortable with making a further effort to resolve the issue themselves. This is YOUR decision and only you can determine what step(s) to take next.

> If at any time you feel threatened by your boss or your boss retaliates in some way for bringing this subject up, you should **take immediate action** with an appropriate department/authority at your place of business. You may also want to consider legal advice if this happens.

In today's business environment it would be rare for a boss not to make an effort to change an inappropriate behavior if you approached him/her in the manner described above. Most bosses are fully aware of the consequences of being accused of harassing or discriminatory behavior. However, if another meeting is called for because the behavior has not changed, then you need to take it to the next level.

Let him know how you feel again, but don't mince words. He needs to understand that this is a serious concern.

> "John, last month I came in and discussed with you what I considered to be a very serious personal issue. I do not feel that your behavior has changed and I am very concerned. I feel that if we can't agree on how to resolve this issue, I will have to take this to the next level."

Let him know that you have been continuing to document your concerns.

> "Since the last time we met about this personal issue, I have noted and documented several additional occasions when I felt your approach to me was demeaning and had sexual overtones."

Then, be willing to detail these incidences, complete with dates, times, verbiage, etc.

Strongly indicate your intention to follow through if the behavior doesn't improve immediately

> "I don't want to take this any further, but if I feel I must, I will contact Human Resources immediately if I am still uncomfortable with what is happening.

If you are very concerned at this point, it may be appropriate to have a trusted person attend this second meeting with you, or possibly include a legal representative.

Follow-through

If your boss still doesn't seem to get the message, then you need to follow through IMMEDIATELY and contact an appropriate agency and/or authority at your place of work. You may very well want to get some legal advice at this stage. A good lawyer, qualified in this area, can help you make the right decisions to take the appropriate actions.

Be aware that an individual may back off for a day or two, or a week or two and then go right back to their highly inappropriate behavior pattern. At this point, you should immediately follow through by reporting this behavior to an appropriate authority and department (Human Resources, legal department, etc.).

Important

I have handled a number of these types of complaints in my work as a manager and as a mentor/coach. I have never had an employee/ client have to take these issues past the stage of initial contact with the perpetrator. When handled in this way, the person got the message loud and clear and the behavior stopped immediately. Sincere apologies, coupled with extreme embarrassment, were part of these resolutions.

> On a number of occasions my clients requested my presence at a meeting with their perpetrator and I served as a mediator. Though there was a good bit of tension to start with, the dialogue served to ease everyone's concerns. Resolutions were reached and the concerns were never raised again.

Yes, you do have the legal right to pursue these types of concerns, and you definitely should if you feel that is the best choice for you. Be aware that this can be very difficult and stressful for everyone concerned. If your boss responds appropriately and makes an effort to change his/her behavior toward you (and others), move ahead with your life and work and be thankful that there are laws and sensibilities today that keep these types of concerns from escalating.

Very important

Your safety and well-being, as well as the safety and well-being of all those who work with you, is of paramount importance. When in doubt, take the actions that are best for you and others.

Questions and Ideas for Contemplation

Repercussions because of even an initial attempt to deal with this type of situation are possible from an egotistical, uncaring, unethical boss. Maintain your vigilance and document any concerns that may arise as a result. Though these would likely be rare if you keep things as open and professional as possible, there really are some jerks in the workplace.

Take care of yourself during any time you are dealing with unethical, inappropriate behavior. It can be a very stressful time. Support and understanding from friends and relatives is particularly helpful. I believe that sharing your concerns with a trusted relative or friend is essential throughout this whole process. This is a very heavy burden to carry alone. A professional personal coach can also provide you with valuable assistance in supporting you through this process, and be a reliable witness if you need one.

Chapter 30

MOVING UP THE CHAIN

Management from both sides

Throughout your work-life you will have many roles. You may be an employee, a line or matrix manager, team leader, and eventually a senior leader. Each of these roles requires slightly different approaches because the dynamics of each situation are different and the relationships you have with people along the chain are different.

In this chapter we will consider how *The Seven Keys to Understanding and Working with Difficult People* can help you with a diversity of roles and perspectives. Some ideas will be reiterated and re-emphasized from earlier in this work, while others will be a slight change in perspective of how you can look at a given situation.

You will find a good many unanswered questions in this chapter. Take some time to answer them for yourself. You will gain a good bit of self-understanding through the process.

Self-awareness

How do you adjust to working in different roles?

Most of us use a slightly different persona when we are in significantly different roles. Some people, especially 'difficult people' as you are probably well aware, change their approach depending on who they are dealing with (and at what level the person is).

> A bullying manager may become a lamb, wimp, obsequious 'servant' to people above him in the chain.
>
> He may be polite and condescending to colleagues that are more or less on the same level as he is.

Knowing what changes take place when <u>you</u> are in differing roles can help you deal successfully at all levels and in the many relationships you have at work.

Knowing how others (above, below, and equal to you in the chain of command) react to your changing persona can be especially illuminating.

Through careful self-observation, you can learn to make adjustments to how you interact with others regardless of their level or relationship with you at work. When you can do this in a positive, open way, you can effect many changes that benefit you, others and your team. Your boss WILL notice.

Through careful self-examination you can observe how you feel about yourself and others in relationship to changes in roles and changes in situations.

Self-worth

How do you FEEL about yourself when you are working in differing roles?

It is very common for us to have our self-worth significantly impacted by not only our role and how it fits into the relationships around us, but by other individuals at work and their roles and approaches.

> Do you feel differently when interacting with a colleague, your boss, an employee?

Are you more in-tune with your true values and self-confidence when you are working with colleagues and team members than in your relationship with your boss?

When you work with employees can you recognize differences in 'the balance of power' and how situations and relationships unfold? Are you maintaining your self-worth or do you become 'bossy' and feel the need to control things?

What are the basic values you want to bring to the table with everyone you interact with at work? It is valuable to write these out and keep them handy. [See exercise in Chapter II, "Self-Awareness.]

What persona is the true you? The one you would like everyone at work to recognize and discuss behind your back? [A good exercise is to write out a variety of statements by others that reflect how you want them to see you.]

> "You know, Ellen is one person you can trust with anything."

> "Go to Ellen if you want it done right."

> "Ellen's a pistol, she is always right in there pitching in when someone needs help."

What do you want them to say about you?

When we can maintain our center focused on the values and qualities we hold closest to our heart, we can maintain healthy relationships with everyone we interact with at work, regardless of position or level.

Self-confidence

When you interact with employees, colleagues, and bosses, is there any change in how well you feel you can handle the situation?

It is fairly common for most people to feel a little anxiety shift in working with people at different levels in an organization. When we can keep on top of our feelings and thoughts, we can make adjustments to our approach that helps solidify our actions in spite of the feelings and slight misgivings we may have.

Our aim is to be able to recognize our thoughts and feelings when we work with people at different levels in our organization, so that we can take control of reactions that may be detrimental to our success and well-being and to make wiser choices for ourselves. If we keep using these self-observation and self-control skills and techniques, then over time our thoughts and feelings, our positive self-worth, self-control, and self-confidence will improve.

Observe how confident you feel when dealing with different people at work. Some people tend to have personalities that affect us more than others. As you stay alert as to how you feel, you will begin to affect your overall self-confidence with everyone. By paying attention we can make an effort to change ourselves when we start to feel uncomfortable – we can learn assertiveness and self-confidence.

Self-control

Are you able to maintain a similar in-control approach to people who hold differing roles in your organization or are all bets off when you have to deal with a high-level manager and/or 'difficult' person?

As you have realized in working through this book to this point, one of the major goals is to learn to control your feelings and reactions in difficult encounters so that you can **respond** in ways that are more positive for everyone involved. When these techniques become part of your repertoire, you will find that these difficult situations and relationships can change dramatically for the better.

A key point in staying on top of your own responses in relationship to differing dynamics at work is to pay attention to whether what you do and say reflects your deepening commitment to self-control or whether you are trying to control the other person and/or the situation. The only true control we can have in our work and life is self-control. Control of others is an illusion and only creates more frustration for everyone.

When you find your feelings, frustrations, and thoughts threatening to take over, can you step back in your mind and make an instantaneous decision to STOP yourself so that you can consider other choices?

What type of person, personality, situation, affects your self-control the most?

Can you identify specific behaviors or issues that you are especially sensitive to?

Honesty

Are you 'in integrity' in all of your relationships at work? (Perkins)

Honesty and integrity go hand in hand. It is critical for us to maintain who we are and how we approach things at all times to all people at all levels.

Things to watch for:

How we see/interact with people at different levels at work.

Do our communications change in scope, depth, and openness simply because a person is above or below us in the chain of command?

'Need to know' can be an important issue at work. Honesty must be considered within the parameters of what is allowed.

However, consider this: it is more honest and open to tell someone that you are restricted in providing them with some information than to keep the information from them by not saying anything at all.

Kindness

How do you treat the people at work that you interact with?

Can you find ways to be kind,

regardless of the circumstances?

When you have something concerning or negative to communicate, can you figure out the kindest means of imparting that concern?

It is always possible to find kind and compassionate ways to say things. It does take training and practice. There are examples throughout this text, but you may want to get some additional practice. Many personal coaches are skilled at these types of communication techniques.

Kindness is an attitude we carry with us throughout the day.

Kindness is a skill we can practice.

Kindness is who we can be at any moment in time if we choose.

Kindness says everything about who we are to other people. How do you want to be seen?

Compassion is kindness in action

in the most difficult of circumstances. (Koob)

Everyone appreciates kindness: don't forget the custodians, administrative assistants, your boss, your boss' boss, your customers, and so on.

Couple kindness with compassion and you have an incredible formula for success.

Positivity

Positivity is a choice we can make every minute of every day.

It is a choice we **can** make with others whenever we interact with them.

It is a choice we **can** make in spite of their negativity.

It is a choice that **can** make the most incredible difference in your work and life.

Choose wisely.

Questions and Ideas for Contemplation

Using *The Seven Keys to Being Successful with Difficult People* as guideposts at work is one way we can effectively change the dynamics of an office. There are many ways you can look at how you interact with others and how that affects your life and work. Use what works for you. Ultimately, however, it is fairly basic:

We are willing to take responsibility for our own life and our work life...

Or

We blame others.

We choose Positivity...

Or

We choose something else.

Chapter 31

MAKING A DIFFERENCE

You can make a difference!

I have been in the 'helping' business for some time now as a mentor, personal and executive coach, and as a caring manager. I imagine my work in this arena has been simply an outgrowth of my personality and my being a consummate educator. Over the span of many years I have seen many people make a difference in their lives and in the lives of the people they interacted with. Sometimes it was with my help, sometimes it was in spite of my own eccentricities. It always involved a willingness for that person to 'take the bull by the horns' and make some life changes.

More than anything else, I have tried these ideas and techniques in my own life. Sometimes it was learning by trial and error. Sometimes the school of hard knocks slowly beat it into my head. At other times, I learned by research, study, understanding, experimentation, choices, and hard self-work.

The results

I enjoy my life more than I ever have in the past. That doesn't mean my life is without worries, trials, tribulations, and the typical concerns we all face. It mostly means I have learned to deal with them better and more positively. I try to take a proactive approach to my life that rests all the responsibility on my own shoulders. I don't always succeed, but I'm getting there.

Also, I don't run into as many difficult people anymore; and the few I run into don't seem so difficult.

That might be because I have learned to deal with them better...or

That I don't see them as being as difficult as I used to...or.

I have more compassion for the eccentricities and differences of others...

Or life just doesn't have to throw them in my path anymore.

I find ways to be successful with almost everyone I deal with – difficult or not. The understanding and skills in this book are relevant to all our relationships and interactions with others.

Yes, I still make mistakes; I am not always as positive as I would like to be; I occasionally let things and other people still get to me; I don't take all the opportunities that are presented to me to be kind and compassionate – I am still learning, too.

The time to start is NOW!

You can make a difference to someone's life (and your own life) right now. The next person you interact with is an opportunity to:

Learn more about yourself.

Learn more about others.

Learn how these ideas, skills, techniques, and tools work

Learn about life and how it works

Learn what a difference Kindness makes

Learn how positivity can turn your whole world around

Be human

Your next opportunity is only the next person away.

Questions and Ideas for Contemplation

You may want to keep reminding yourself that your difficult boss is a person, too!

Chapter 32

MAKING THE MOST OF YOUR LIFE AND WORK

How do you feel at Work?

Tired, Frustrated, Depressed, Angry, Un-motivated, Dis-spirited,

Beaten up, Ignored, Un-appreciated, Stymied,

Un-recognized, Un-rewarded, Unhappy

OR

Fulfilled, Peaceful, Motivated, Energetic,

Uplifted; Supported; Appreciated;

Recognized; Rewarded; Happy

Who do you blame?

'Them,' Your Colleagues, 'The Team,' The Organization, Circumstances, Life,

Your Boss?

Excuses only Cheat...**YOU**

Take your life back from 'THEM'

"The first Rule of Holes: if you are in one, STOP DIGGING!"

(Molly Ivins)

Are you digging holes today or building something?

Sometimes all it takes besides getting out of the hole we are in is building something small ¥¥ like reconnecting a damaged relationship, touching a person we care about, putting a smile on a co-workers face ¥¥ that makes ALL the difference in our world and theirs. Start building today. You don't need to build a castle, you just need to dream a little.

This is YOUR life

You are the ONLY one who can make a difference every day!

You CAN make a difference in your relationship with your boss, with your colleagues, with the total experience you have at work. The most important decision you can make is to commit yourself to making that difference and to give up relying on others to change or do it for you. TODAY is the day you can start.

Everything we do and say to others affects their day and ours,

And even more importantly HOW we say and do it.

Be proactive with your difficult boss

All the choices you make every time you interact with your boss, either directly or indirectly through your work, impact your relationship with him/her.

Keep this important point in mind: the more critical, blaming, demanding, 'difficult' a person is, the more desperate is his/her craving for attention. By understanding your boss' needs, wants, and desires you can make a major difference in how they perceive you, how they interact with you, and how they treat you.

"Turn setbacks into chances to improve things." (William Bridges)

How we approach difficulties determines who we are as an employee, a person, as a human being. It also sets up a completely different perception in others of who we are and how we approach our work.

Be a Champion

By being:

There for others

Proactive

Solution-Oriented

Kind and Compassionate

A dispenser of Enthusiasm

True to YOURSELF

If you are not having FUN in Your Life -

Try Something Else.

If you are not having FUN – Adjust!

What you have going for YOU

Intelligence

Curiosity

Caring

Creativity

Ability to learn (every day)

Ability to Communicate – Kindly and Wisely

Ability to Understand others

And so much more.

You have the wisdom of invaluable years of experience

Including...

Experience with difficult people

What have you learned from them?

More importantly, **what ARE you learning from them now?**

"The most important measure of how good a game I played

was how much better I made my teammates play."

(Bill Russell, Basketball Star)

Negative versus Positive

Far too often we focus on the negatives, difficulties, concerns we have in life and don't take enough time for the good things:

Celebrate what's Right with the World!

(National Geographic)

Live YOUR life OUT LOUD!

(Zola, Peters)

CHOICES

I am going to worry all the time and kick myself whenever I do something

that is remotely stupid.

I am going to feel bad whenever anyone puts me down, be depressed

because no one likes me, and get frustrated all the time

because no one listens to me.

I am not going to take care of myself when I get tired, over-worked, or ill

or take time for myself because I have way too much to do.

I am going to accept everything bad that anyone says about me,

because it's all true.

I am going to wallow in self-pity.

Or

I am going to stop worrying and look at the brighter side of life.

I am going to pay attention to my thoughts and feelings and when I start to
think negatively or to kick myself,

I am going to turn my thoughts around and say supportive,

kind things to myself.

I am going to be self-confident, believe in myself, and maintain a calm, cool, collected persona wherever I am and with whomever I am with.

I am going to be assertive, kind, and compassionate in all my dealings

with others.

I am going to pay attention to my communications and always try to present

a positive me to the rest of the world.

I am going to believe in myself.

Difficultpeople.org

BIBLIOGRAPHIES

Difficult People Books by Dr. Joseph Koob

Annotated Bibliography

Understanding and Working with Difficult People

We believe this book presents the most comprehensive material available about being successful with difficult people. This book is designed to be a practical, accessible introduction to the very broad topic of dealing with difficult people/difficult behaviors. Since every difficult situation is different, the focus here will be on building a basic understanding of how you interact with difficult people, what makes difficult people tick, and the most fundamental skills you can bring to the table to help change these encounters for the better.

ME! A Difficult Person?

This is second of our signature books. This book focuses on learning more about yourself. Most of us are occasionally difficult or seen as difficult by others. This may simply be a matter of different perspectives, or it may mean that we have some inner work to do. This course is concerned with understanding more about how you come across to others, and understanding more about who you are as a person. It is also concerned with self-improvement – making changes that will help make your interactions with others significantly better, and that will bring you more peace, comfort, and joy in your life.

Difficult Spouses? Improving and Saving Your Relationship with Your Significant Other

Are you having difficulties in your current relationship? Facing a divorce? Newly divorced and trying to understand what happened and what you could have done about it? We feel this book has value not only for couples who are simply having difficulties in their relationships with their significant others, but also those facing divorce, recently divorced couples, and for people entering new relationships. The focus is on developing the knowledge, skills, and tools to help your relationship be successful.

Dealing with Difficult Strangers

Being successful in difficult situations with strangers is all about what you can bring to the situation. You will find a tremendous amount of useful information and skills included in this book that can make a significant difference in how you approach difficult strangers, how you feel as a result of these difficult encounters, and how you can emerge without a negative experience having ruined your day.

Succeeding with Difficult Professors (and Tough Courses)

A course for college students at all levels. What you need to know to make the most of your college career. This course has two main sections: "Getting along with Difficult Professors," and "Succeeding in Tough Classes." The first section will discuss ideas and skills you can use to get through personal difficulties with professors. The second section will focus on techniques, study skills, and approaches that will help you get the grades you want.

Guiding Children

Guiding and working with children is on the mind of every parent. This book focuses on skills and tools to help you as a parent provide the best possible environment for your child's development by avoiding difficulties through intelligent upbringing. This book is not only about helping you to guide your children through concerns that arise, but it is even more about enjoying your children. They do grow up, much faster than we expect. Take advantage of the tremendous joy they can bring into your life and the vast understanding of life that they provide. You will be glad you did.

Dealing with Difficult Customers

(for Employees, Companies, and Customer Service Personnel)

This book is all about putting the gamut of customer relations and interactions into a perspective that is workable, livable, and supports you, the customer contact person, throughout.

While many businesses do provide extensive customer relations training, the focus is often fairly one way – aimed at keeping business. We present you with extensive insight and knowledge about the customer's perspective, what you need to know as a company representative to fulfill your job, the internal and external support you need, and the tools and skills to communicate effectively with difficult customers.

Caring for Difficult Patients: A Guide for Nursing Professionals

I believe that the Nursing profession is one of the most admired in America. We think of Nurses as professional: that is, they have a knowledge base and skill set that is unique and valued – the quality of their work is important to them; and we think of Nurses as people who care about their patients – they are concerned with our well-being when we are under their care. These considerations are the focal point for discussing how to best deal with difficult patients

Trilogy: Dealing with Change

Books centered on Leaders working through change:

Difficult Situations - Dealing with Change

Change and difficult situations can certainly produce a great deal of angst, and as a result, difficult people. This book focuses on learning the skills and tools you need to deal with the ongoing stresses of constant change in the business world today. It is about knowledgeable leadership: how what you do helps you get through change, and more importantly helps you lead others through change. It presumes you are already inspired, good, intelligent, and practical. This book is about making a difference.

Honoring Work and Life: 99 Words for Leaders to Live By

This book provides a foundation of key ideas that focus on Leadership and Personal qualities, attributes, and behaviors that honor not only our work but our life. It is my firm belief that true leaders work to serve their fellow employees, their team, their company, their customers, as well as their families and friends. This is about understanding and working on those attributes that make great leaders.

Leaders Managing Change

Leaders Managing Change is about understanding and dealing with the ongoing stresses of constant change in the business world today, but most importantly it is about leadership. When I thought about the concerns that are a regular part of high turnover rates, leadership changes, acquisitions and mergers, and the myriad of other transitions businesses face today, the focus came down to leadership. Good leaders get things done. This book focuses on knowledgeable leadership (i.e. what you need to know to help you deal with change as a leader). It presumes you are already inspired, good, intelligent, and practical. This book is about making a difference.

Business Trilogy

Dealing with Difficult Coworkers

The emphasis here is on helping people solve the difficulties they have at work with someone who is relatively speaking a 'coworker,' or 'colleague,' in other words, someone whose 'rank' or 'job' is roughly on the same level as yours. Are you perturbed, exasperated, frustrated, angry, upset, and genuinely peeved with someone at work? We have all had occasion to work with someone who seems to have a wide range of concerns with other people in the workplace. Can we succeed with them and turn a difficult situation around? Can we enjoy our work-life once again? Definitely! This book provides you with key ideas, skills, and tools that you can use to be successful with difficult colleagues. The power is in your own inner strength and the knowledge and understanding you develop.

Succeeding with Difficult Bosses

Have a tough boss? This is a practical, in-the-trenches approach to succeeding with a difficult authority figure – a (how to) book for one of your most important relationships at work. This book is specifically focused on understanding the unique relationship we have with a person who has hierarchical power over us. To truly gain the knowledge we need to be successful with difficult bosses, we need to understand who they are as a person and what they do that frustrates us. We must also understand ourselves – how we subconsciously add to the mix, and how we can change our outlook and behavior so that our boss will change his/her behavior in relationship to us. When people talk about 'difficult' bosses, the root of their concerns is often that they FEEL left out, unappreciated, put down, 'less than,' i.e., treated almost as a non-entity. If you feel this way, this book was written for you

Managing Difficult Employees

This book is about what YOU as a manager and leader bring to the table. It addresses two key questions: Is your leadership conducive to a positive work environment with few personnel concerns; and, when concerns do arise, are you prepared to handle them effectively and efficiently? The first part of this book focuses on avoiding difficulties through knowledgeable and inspired leadership. Part II of this work will demonstrate how to apply your personal strengths and your management and leadership skills to working successfully with difficult personnel concerns and in difficult situations.

Difficult People Materials

Axelrod, A and Holtje, J., *201 Ways to Deal with Difficult People*, McGraw-Hill, New York, 1997.

Bell, A. and Smith, D., *Winning with Difficult People*, Barron's, New York, 1997

Bramson, Robert M., *Coping with Difficult Bosses*, Fireside, New York, 1992.

Bramson, Robert M., *Coping with Difficult People*, Anchor Press, New York, 1981.

Braunstein, Barbara, *How to Deal with Difficult People*, Skillpath Publications, Mission, KS, 1994. [Tapes]

Brinkman, R. and Kirschner, R., *Dealing with People You Can't Stand,* McGraw-Hill, New York, 1994.

Carter, Jay, *Nasty Bosses: How to STOP BEING HURT by them without stooping to THEIR level*, McGraw-Hill, New York, 2004.

Case, Gary and Rhoades-Baum, *How to Handle Difficult Customers*, Help Deck Institute, Colorado Springs, 1994.

Cava, Roberta, *Dealing with Difficult People: How to Deal with Nasty Customers, Demanding Bosses and Annoying Co-workers*, Firefly Books, Buffalo, NY, 2004.

Cava, Roberta, *difficult people: How to Deal with Impossible clients, Bosses, and Employees*, Firefly Books, Buffalo, NY, 1990.

Cavaiola, A. And Lavender, N., *Toxic Coworkers: How to Deal with Dysfunctional People on the Job*, New Harbinger Publications, Oakland, CA, 2000.

Costello, Andrew, *How to Deal with Difficult People*, Ligori Publications, Liguri, MI, 1980.

Crowe, Sandra, *Since Strangling Isn't An Option*, Perigee, New York, 1999.

Diehm, William, *How to Get Along with Difficult People*, Broadman Press, Nashville, 1992.

207

Felder, Leonard, *Does Someone Treat You Badly? How to Handle Brutal Bosses, Crazy Coworkers...and Anyone Else Who Drives You Nuts*, Berkley Books, NY, 1993.

First, Michael, Ed., *Diagnostic and Statistical Manual for Mental Disorders*, 4th Edition, American Psychiatric Asso.,Washington, 1994.

Friedman, Paul, *How to Deal with Difficult People*, SkillPath Publications, Mission, KS, 1994.

Gill, Lucy, *How to Work with Just About Anyone*, Fireside, New York, 1999.

Griswold, Bob, *Coping with Difficult and Negative People and Personal Magnetism*, Effective Learning Systems, Inc., Edina, MN. [Tape]

Holloway, Andy, "Bad Boss Blues," *Canadian Business*, 24 Oct 2004.

Hoover, John, *How to Work for an Idiot: Survive & Thrive Without Killing Your Boss*, Career Press, Princeton, NJ, 2004.

Jones, Katina, *Succeeding with Difficult People*, Longmeadow Press, Stamford, CT, 1992.

Keating, Charles, *Dealing with Difficult People*, Paulist Press, New York, 1984.

Littauer, Florence, *How to Get Along with Difficult People*, Harvest House, Eugene, 1984.

Lloyd, Ken, *Jerks at Work: How to Deal with People Problems and Problem People*, Career Press, Franklin Lakes, NJ, 1999

Lundin, W. and Lundin, J., *When Smart People Work for Dumb Bosses: How to Survive in a Crazy and Dysfunctional Workplace*, McGraw-Hill, New York, 1998.

Markham, Ursula, *How to deal with Difficult people*, Thorsons, London, 1993.

Meier, Paul, *Don't Let Jerks Get the Best of You: Advice for Dealing with Difficult People*, Thomas Nelson, Nashville, 1993.

Namie, G. and Namie, R., *the Bully at Work*, Sourcebooks, Inc., Naperville, IL, 2000.

Osbourne, Christina, *Dealing with Difficult People*, DK, London, 2002.

Oxman, Murray, *The How to Easily Handle Difficult People, Success Without Stress*, Morro Bay, CA, 1997.

Perkins, Betty, *Lion Taming: The Courage to Deal with Difficult People Including Yourself*, Tzedakah Publications, Scramento, 1995.

Rosen, Mark, *Thank You for Being Such A Pain: Spiritual Guidance for Dealing with Difficult People*, Three Rivers Press, New York, 1998.

Segal, Judith, *Getting Them to See It Your Way: Dealing with Difficult and Challenging People*, Lowell House, Los Angeles, 2000.

Solomon, Muriel, *Working with Difficult People*, Prentice Hall, Englewood Cliffs,1990.

Toropov, Brandon, *The Complete Idiot's Guide to Getting Along with Difficult People*, Alpha Books, New York, 1997.

Toropov, Brandon, *Manager's Guide to Dealing with Difficult People*, Prentice Hall, Paramus, NJ, 1997.

Turecki, Stanley, *The Difficult Child*, Bantam Books, NY, 1989.

Weiner, David L., *Power Freaks: Dealing with Them in the Workplace or Anywhere*, Prometheus Books, Amherst, New York, 2002

Weiss, Donald, *How to Deal with Difficult People*, Amacon, New York, 1987.

Recommended Readings

Dewey, John, *Democracy and Education*, Norwood Press, Norwood, MA, 1916.

Dewey, John, *Education and Experience*, Kappa Delta Pi Publications, Macmillian, New York, 1938.

Dyer, Wayne, *Pulling Your Own Strings*, Funk and Wagnalls, New York, 1978.

Dyer, Wayne, *Your Erroneous Zones*, Funk and Wagnalls, New York, 1976.

Dyer, Wayne, *Your Sacred Self*, Harper, New York, 1995.

Guraik, David B., Editor, *Webster's New World Dictionary*, World Publishing, New York, 1972.

Heinlein, Robert, *Time Enough for Love*, New English Library, New York, 1974.

Hesse, Hermann, *Narcissus and Goldmund*, Bantam, New York, 1971.

James, M, and Jongeward, D. *Born to Win*, Addison-Wesley, 1971.

Koob, Joseph, *A Perfect Day: Guide for A Better Life*, NEJS Publications, Lawton, OK, 1998.

Parrott, Thomas Marc, Ed., *Shakespeare: Twenty-three Plays and the Sonnets*, Charles Scribner's Sons, Washington, D.C., 1938.

Pirsig, Robert, *Zen and the Art of Motorcycle Maintenance*, Bantam, New York, 1980.

Rand, Ayn, *Atlas Shrugged*, Signet Books, New York, 1957.

Redman, Ben Ray, Editor, *The Portable Voltaire*, Viking Press, New York, 1949.

Books and other works on Change and Leadership

Bolles, Richard N., *What Color is Your Parachute?* Ten Speed Press, Berkeley, CA, 1987.

Bridges, William, *Managing Transitions: Making the Most of Change*, Perseus Books, Cambridge, 1991.

Bridges, William, *Transitions: Making Sense of Life's Changes*, Perseus Books, Cambridge, 1980.

Buckingham, Marcus, & Coffman, Curt, *First, Break All the Rules: What the World's Greatest Managers Do Differently*, Simon and Schuster, New York, 1999.

Collins, J., and Porras, J., *Built to Last: Successful Habits of Visionary Companies*, Harper Business, NY, 2001.

Collins, Jim, *Good TO Great: Why Some Companies Make the Leap...and Others Don't*, Harper Business, NY, 2001.

Cooper, Robert and Sawaf, Ayman, *Executive EQ: Emotional Intelligence in Leadership & Organizations*, Grisset/Putnam, New York, 1996.

Crane, Thomas, *The Heart of Coaching*, FTA Press, San Diego, 1998.

Deits, Bob, Life *After Loss: A Personal Guide Dealing with Death, Divorce, Job Change and Relocation*, Fisher Books, Tucson, 1988.

Dominhguez, Linda R., *How to Shine at Work*, McGraw Hill, 2003.

Drucker, Peter F., *Managing in a Time of Great Change*, Truman Talley Books, NY, 1995.

Evard, Beth L. And Gipple, Craig A., *Managing Business Change for Dummies*, Hungry Minds, Inc., NY,2001.

Farson, Richard and Keyes, Ralph, *Whoever Makes the Most Mistakes Wins: The Paradox of Innovation*, Free Press, NY, 2002.

Fortgang, Laura Berman, *Take Yourself to the Top: The Secrets of America's #1 Career Coach*, Warner Books, New York, 1998.

Gates, Bill, *Business @ the Speed of Thought: Succeeding in the Digital Economy*, Warner Books, New York, 1999.

Gerstner, Jr., Louis, V, *Who Says Elephants Can't Dance? Leading a Great Enterprise Through Dramatic Change*, HarperBusiness, New York, 2002.

Going Through Bereavement—When a loved one dies, Langeland Memorial Chapel, Kalamazoo, MI.

Grieve, Bradly T., *The Blue Day Book: A Lesson in Cheering Yourself Up*, Andrews McMeel Publishing, Kansas City, 2000.

Goldratt, Eliyahu M., *Critical Chain*, North River Press, Great Barrington, MA, 1997.

Hammer, Michael and Champy, James, *Reengineering the Corporation: A Manifesto for Business Revolution, HarperBusiness*, New York, 1993.

Hoffer, Eric, *The Ordeal of Change*, Harper & Row, NY, 1952.

Jeffreys, J. Shep. *Coping with Workplace Change: Dealing with Loss and Grief*, Crisp Productions, Menlo Park, CA, 1995.

Johnson, Spencer, *Who Moved My Cheese*, G. P. Putnam, New York, 1998.

Kanter, Rosabeth Moss, *The Change Masters: Innovation & Entrepreneurship in the American Corporation*, Simon & Schuster, New York, 1983.

Kelley, Robert, *How to be a Star at Work: Nine Breakthrough Strategies You Need to Succeed*, Random House, New York, 1998.

Koob, Joseph E. II, *Difficult Situations: Dealing with Change*, NEJS Publications, Saline, MI, 2004.

Kotter, John P, *Leading Change*, Harvard Business School Press, Boston, 1996.

Kotter, John P, *The Leadership Factor*, Free Press, New York, 1988.

Kouzes, J. and Posner, B., *Credibility: How Leaders Gain and Lose it; Why People Demand it*, Jossey-Bass Publishers, San Francisco, 1993.

Kuster, Elizabeth, *Exorcising Your Ex*, Fireside, New York, 1996.

Leonard, George, *Mastery: The Keys to Success and Long-term Fulfillment*, Plume, NY 1992.

Lunden, Joan, and Cagan, Andrea, *A Bend in the Road is Not the End of the Road,* William Morrow, New York, 1998.

Maxwell, John C., *The 21 Indispensible Qualities of Leadership: Becoming the Person Others Will Want to Follow*, Thomas Nelson Publishers, Nashville, 1999.

Maxwell, John C., *The 17 Indisputable Laws of Teamwork: Embrace them and Empower Your Team*, Thomas Nelson Publishers, Nashville, 2001.

Maxwell, John C., *21 Irrefutable Laws of Leadership*, Thomas Nelson, Inc., Nashville, 1998.

Milwid, Beth, *Working With Men: Professional Women Talk About Power, Sexuality, and Ethics*, Beyond Words, Kingsport, TN, 1990.

McKay, Harvey, *Swim with the Sharks: Without Being Eaten Alive*, William Morrow Co., New York, 1988.

Messer, Bonnie J., *Dealing with Chan*ge, Abington Press, 1996.

Montalbo, Thomas, *The Power of Eloquence: Magic Key to Success in Public Speaking*, Prentive-Hall, Englewood Cliffs, N.J., 1984.

Pasternack, Bruce and Viscio, Albert, *The Centerless Corporation: A New Model for Transforming Your Organization for Growth and Prosperity*, Fireside, New York, 1998.

Peters, Tom, *The Circle of Innovation: You Can't Shrink Your Way to Greatnness*, Vintage Books, New York, 1999.

Peters, Tom, *Liberation Management: Necessary Disorganization for the Nanosecond Nineties*, Faucett Columbine, New York, 1992.

Peters, Tom, and Waterman, Robert, *In Search of Excellence: Lessons from America's Best-Run Companies*, Harper & Row, New York, 1982.

Peters, Tom, and Austin, Nancy, *A Passion for Excellence: The Leadership Difference*, Random House, New York, 1985.

Peters, Tom, *The Pursuit of WOW! Every Person's Guide to Topsy-Turvy Times*, Vintage Books, New York, 1994.

Peters, Tom, *Professional Service Firm 50: Fifty Ways to Transform Your "Department" into a Professional Service Firm whose Trademarks are Passion and Excellence*, Alfred A. Knopf, 1999.

Peters, Tom, *Re-imagine! Business Excellence in a Disruptive Age*, DK, London, 2003.

Peters, Tom, *Thriving on Chaos: Handbook for a Management Revolution*, Alfred Knopf, New York, 1987

Popcorn, Faith, *EVEolutuon: The Eight Truths of Marketing to Women*, Hyperion Books, 2001.

Smith, Hyrum W. The *10 Natural Laws of Successful Time and Life Management: Proven Strategies for Increased Productivity and Inner Peace*, Warner Books, New York, 1994.

Talbot, Kay, *The Ten Biggest Myths About Grief*, Abbey Press, St. Meinrad, IN, 2000.

Waterman, Robert H., Jr., *The Renewal Factor: How The Best Get And Keep The Competitive Edge*, Bantam, New York, 1986.

Whitmore, John, *Coaching for Performance*, Nicholas Brealey Publishing, London, 1999.